GASP!

You Will Spend Forever Somewhere: How to Make Sure It's Heaven

Tony Nolan

PS.147:3

GASP!
You Will Spend Forever Somewhere: How to Make Sure It's Heaven
by Tony Nolan

Printed in the United States of America

ISBN 9781619046337

www.xulonpress.com

This book is a gift to:

...Because forever is a long time,

and I want to make sure

we enjoy it together.

Contents

Introduction

What on earth caused me to title this book, "GASP!"? Actually, it wasn't anything on earth that inspired me. It was a phenomenon, a supernatural event, which could have a profound impact on *your* destiny. (I'm sorry—I know I just kind of took a big leap into your space; but what I know, compels me to do so.) You see, I've been given some insights, possibly about your future that forced me to write a book called, "GASP!" Well, I'm getting ahead of myself, here. (People with a prescience about the fate of others, tend to do that.) Let's go back to answering the question asked earlier. Understand that unwrapping this little mystery is going to take some participation on your part, too.

To start our journey together through this book, I will need your vocal and breathing skills. Let's start by reading the title one more time, "GASP!" Now, here is where your involvement comes in to-play. To "gasp" means to draw in your breath sharply, as from shock. You've heard someone gasp before, haven't you? When a person gasps, he opens his mouth and rapidly inhales air, which races across his vocal cords, creating a loud howling vortex. Now, with that in mind, it's time for you to kick in your vocal-breathing skills. On the count of three, I want you to do your best and loudest gasp ever! (I know what you are thinking, "Tony, did you just ask me to gasp out loud?" Yes, I did. And I *want* it to be loud: *really* loud.) If you have people around you, please don't worry about what they will think, when they hear you gasp. Make something up when they look at you, like saying, "Wow, this is a great book!" (Just go with this; work with me here!) Get ready to do your best gasp ever. Here we go. Are you ready? —Okay, on the count of three, 1...2...3! "GASP!" Very good! (Did you really do it? If you did—and I hope you did—I wish I could have been there to see you do it!)

At this point in the book, you've got to be questioning my sanity. You're probably thinking, "Tony, this is the craziest opening to any book I have ever read. As a matter of fact, I don't think I've ever been asked by an author to gasp out loud, while reading. I bought this book, hoping it would have some sort of spiritual significance in my life, and this is how it starts - with an exercise in gasping? What in the world could that possibly have to do with my spirituality?" First of all, I'd like to make it clear that I understand how someone could feel this way about the opening of the book. It does seem a bit weird, and if you're reading this while waiting for your turn at a dentist's office, you probably got more than a few interesting looks. (Perhaps you even made some children cry, who were already on-edge, because of that drilling-noise, coming from the other side of the wall.) But, if you track with me here, you will see that the gasp does have a serious spiritual connection. I will go so far as to say, there is a significant relation between the gasp and your relationship with Almighty God.

How is that possible, and what difference will it make in your life? The joy and empowerment that come from the answers to those questions, will be your reward for taking the journey through this book. Keep reading, and if it helps, I promise that I won't ask you to gasp again. As a matter of fact, it's my desire that by the end of this book, you won't ever be a "gasper." (Oops, there I go again, getting ahead of myself; it's because of what I know.) Let's start by looking at a couple of verses found in the Gospel of Matthew.

Chapter One

Blast Back!

Although I'm not one of those Sci-Fi guys, I am a bit intrigued with time travel. Wouldn't it be cool to have a time-machine? If I had one, I'd use it to travel back in history about two thousand years. It's a point in history, when the modes of transportation were camels and donkeys. There were no convenient stores; instead, you got your milk from the family pet-goat. The fashion trending of that period was tunics, turbans, and sandals. Don't get me wrong, I am not wanting to go back in time, because I'm crazy about those things; not at all. I love my truck, my Levi's, and my Nike shoes. My interest in making this trip, is to catch a specific event that took place. I want to be dropped right in the middle of a crowd that is gathered on a hillside in the Middle East. The masses are huddled together, with their ears dialed-in to something astonishing—and I want to hear it, too.

Since I have not been able to find a time machine (if you have one, please email me), I'll have to get there in my mind. I don't like to travel alone, so I'm inviting you to accompany me on this journey. I know it will be one that changes both of us. So, if you're up for it, let's open up our minds—but don't close your eyes, because you'll need them to read the next paragraph, which is actually going to launch us back into history.—Let's go!

Think weird, Sci-Fi, radio-wave noises; flashes of bright light, with blurred images of objects, racing past our heads; and, voila!— We're there! Take a moment to get your legs back underneath you, and check-out your surroundings. Remember the crowd of people I wanted to be among, listening to something astonishing? We've landed right in the middle of them! The temperature is quite different from where we were in our air-conditioned homes. It's very hot here, as the radiant sun blisters this patch of geography. Thankfully, there is a soft, intermittent breeze, making it tolerable to be outside. The cool wind is helpful, for those on the fringes of this gathering, but not so much for the thousands within its core. (Perhaps that explains why they are frantically erecting tents, trying their best to create some shade, which I'm thinking is a great idea.) The landscape consists of pebble-laden foot trails, snaking along a carpet of lush, green rolling hills, and checkered with clusters of large boulders. If I checked the GPS on my Smartphone, it would indicate that we are at the foot of the Mount of Olives, on the east side of Jerusalem.

The sun is intense now, and I didn't bring my sunblock—nor did you. So, let's squeeze-in under one of those crowded tents, to keep from getting scorched. Huh…my nose has detected a distinct odor, causing me to question the hygiene practices of these Easterners. (My sense of smell isn't quite used to this, but I think it can handle the funk, better than my skin can endure the UV rays. You seem to agree; so, let's stay here, endure the smell and even the rambunctious children at play.) Whoa!—I just got bumped by a small boy, who's chasing his buddy, causing me to stumble into the lady next to me. She is completely shrouded in yards of fabric, making only her eyes visible through the tiny rectangular opening in her veil. From the look she is giving me, her sense of smell is equally appalled at my American cologne. Along with the rest of the crowd, we're going to put up with each other for the moment. It's a small inconvenience to pay, in order for us to hear the greatest Teacher of all time—Jesus of Nazareth.

We have converged to witness the most famous sermon ever preached, The Beatitudes. The murmuring of the crowd begins to fade throughout the congregation, as each person hushes and leans-in, to absorb the words of the Son of God. There are people, who have said Jesus was not much to look at; but everybody agrees: He sure can preach! He did not have an amplification system or any high-definition video screens, to project His talking-points. Most modern-day motivational speakers wouldn't dare try to pull this off without those things, to help arrest the attention of such a large crowd, *especially* in an outdoor venue. Jesus, however, doesn't need any of that technological ear- and eye-candy. He has something extra that sets Him apart from any other speaker in history: He has *authority*! Luke 4:32 says, "And they were astonished at His teaching, for His word was with authority." Matthew 28:18 also records, "All authority in Heaven and on earth has been given to Me."

Aren't you glad you took this time-leap with me? We are about to witness one of the single, most powerful moments in preaching history. There stands Jesus—a hill for His stage; the sun is His spotlight; and nothing but the wind to carry His voice, as He preaches His heart out. He covers a gamut of subjects: from religion, politics, and relationships, to the origin of truth. The people are mesmerized, glued to every word, as Jesus preaches all day!

After hours of soaking-up His teaching and shielding ourselves from the sun, twinkling eyes and soft smiles from many in the crowd advertise their approval. As the sun's blazing fireball begins to slowly drift behind the hill, I find myself smiling with the people, and Jesus is smiling, too. His smile isn't about the shade's relief and temperature-change it brings; His smile is about their souls. He loves every single person within the sound of His voice (and on the face of the whole earth, for that matter). He's been pouring-out His heart, because He wants each of us to be swallowed-up in His great salvation.

As the last glistening, golden ray of light tucks itself beneath the grass line of the hill, the expression on the face of Jesus changes. A look of intense concern replaces His smile. He has one last thing to say to us in this sermon. As the curves of His lips morph into tight, straight lines, His tone alters, and His voice is very different. – This tonal shift is like the situation-contrast of someone in a library, gently assuring another inquiring student that the seat beside her is empty; and a fireman, frantically warning people to escape a burning building. His eyes are ablaze with urgency, as He preaches the words we find penned in the Gospel of Matthew 7:21-23 —

"Not everyone who says to Me, 'Lord, Lord.' shall enter the kingdom of heaven, but he who does the will of My Father in heaven. Many will say to Me in that day, 'Lord, Lord, have we

not prophesied in Your name, cast out demons in Your name, and done many wonders in Your name?' And then I will declare to them, 'I never knew you; depart from Me, you who practice lawlessness!'"

I know we've been imagining the possible realities of this historical event, but —oh, man!—I would love to have been there in that very moment, when His words reverberated across the audience members' eardrums. So, if you're up to it, let's keep mentally painting this masterpiece in time. Continuing to roll with the time-machine idea, let's imagine we actually went back to this moment. (Remember the Smartphone I had, with the GPS on it? Being the gadget-junkie that I am, I made sure it had a camera-feature on it, and I caught the *whole* sermon on video! I have been accused of having a vivid imagination, and, yes—it's in overdrive right about now. Please, don't fault me for it; follow me in it.)

Throughout the rest of this book, we will be rewinding, pausing, and going in slow- motion through the scene-selections of this famous sermon by Jesus. It's my desire that, frame by frame, we will catch significant details that will help us experience and embrace what Jesus was trying to communicate through His message. Oh, by the way—the GASP?—It's in there. What! You didn't see it, as I quoted the verses? Well, don't worry. Most everybody misses it, at first glance. So, let's rewind and take a closer look, because, as I stated earlier, it has *everything* to do with your spirituality.

Chapter Two

Rewind!

A simple flick of the forefinger on the "Rewind" arrow takes us all the way back to the beginning of our adventure in the Middle East. A soft press of the "Play" -button sets the stage for us to re-live the whole event. The picture starts off a bit blurry, but it's not a focus-issue. (The blurs are due to the congestion that was in our tent. Several head coverings keep invading the scope of the lens, blocking out the figure of Jesus; but the audio is good.) Above the murmurs and clatter, the voice of Jesus declares, "Not everyone who says to Me, 'Lord, Lord,' shall enter the kingdom of Heaven, but he who does the will of My Father in Heaven." Pause it! —Did you catch that? Jesus directly stated that there are people, who are not going to enter the kingdom of Heaven. In other words, He is clearly saying that not everyone is going to heaven. That's an alarming news flash for most people. I can tell you, this kind of teaching rubs the pluralistic carpet of our culture the wrong way.

Our globe is saturated with the mindset that all roads lead to Heaven. I encounter people in my travels, who embrace a system of beliefs that all religions are equal, converging into one path leading to God. Then, we have another culture of people that seems to think, if one lives a life of good deeds out-weighing any bad deeds, this will then get a person to Heaven. In the southern region of the United States, there are large sectors of people, which actually believe that their membership and affiliation with a local Baptist church will get them into Heaven. There is also a massive movement of young people around the globe, thinking Heaven can be obtained by working hard to blot-out social injustices, such as poverty, sex-trafficking, or abortion.

The ideas and viewpoints are as diverse and incorrect today, as they were in Jesus' day. Contrary to the thinking of those, who believe everything is going to be okay (because God will let us all into Heaven, based on our deeds, merits or some sort of politically-correct curve), Jesus' words blast that philosophy and worldview. He says the only ones getting into Heaven are those, who do the will of His Father. Those are powerful, definitive words, but what does the phrasing, "...he who does the will of My Father," mean?

What Jesus is teaching is really quite simple to understand. The take-away is that you cannot get into Heaven *your* way. It's God's way, or no way, period! He mentions this in other places in the Bible, as well. In John 14:6, Jesus says, "I am the way, the truth, and the life. No one comes to the Father, except through Me." He was saying there are *not* many ways to God; there is only *one* way, and it's through Him—Jesus Christ. Acts 4:12 states it clearly, "Nor is there salvation in any other, for there is no other name under heaven given among men, by which we must be saved." This is a point worth bearing-down on. I have met and counseled with thousands of people around the world, and my spiritual discussions have led me to some very interesting—yet, disturbing—ideas that aren't in line with Jesus' teachings. Most people think they can get into Heaven some way, other than what Jesus clearly said in the Bible. This mindset often carries itself over from the ordinary things we try to tackle in life. Let me explain.

There are a lot of people, who take shortcuts in life. It's not so much that they don't like being told what to do; they just think they can do things themselves, and everything will turn-out just fine. Students get video games, toss the game guide on the floor, and start tapping buttons on the controller. They play, but it takes a lot longer to win (if they win at all). Women skip a step in the recipe for cooking dinner, in an attempt to hurry. (If you have tasted some of that nasty chicken, you know this shortcut could royally screw-up a dinner.) The point Jesus is making here is much more important, because it can jack-up a soul—forever!

Where we primarily see this whole mindset of "do it myself" or "my own way" surface is in the lives of men. We guys tend to think we don't need instructions to put something together. We have some sort of delusional strand in our DNA that tells our brains that we are very capable of taking complex instruction-feats and pulling-them-off without one ounce of help from an instruction manual. I vividly recall a man-moment I had, while assembling a swing-set that I purchased for my children. (As I type this on my laptop, I am reminded of this encounter because my fingers, which are necessary for typing, don't quite function as they did, before I went to war with that play-set. Did I say, "War?" Yes, I did. And I will now tell you why.)

I one day stood staring at a massive pile of wood and screws in my backyard. With a strong desire to conquer and a heart swelling with a passion to make my kids smile, I was ready to take-on this challenge. Blood was already dripping from a wound I received from getting the pieces out of the box. (What relative of Jig-Saw had the idea to design a box that's held together by razor-sharp, copper staples? He should be imprisoned for an act of terrorism!) The front of the box had a picture of what the swing-set was supposed to look like. However, due to my fight with the box, the picture was shredded into a million little pieces. I tried to reconstruct the picture, by collecting the pieces and putting them together like a puzzle. The whimsical wind was often a problem in this process, but that little DNA-strand was convincing me that I had a photographic memory and everything would be fine.

There was a folded chunk of paper that came with the set, and it had the word "Instructions" printed on the side of it. However, they were wrapped in so much clear packing-tape, I don't think I could have opened it, even if I would have wanted to. That was the problem, though: *I did not want to.* I am a man, and my brain was telling me that I could actually put this thing together in the dark, blind-folded, without hands, and without the need to breathe. My sliced hand was screaming for a bandage (which I did not put on, because my man-nerve thought that it would be better to bleed-to-death, than to be seen with a dressed-wound that I had received from unwrapping a toy). Feeling a little woozy from the blood-loss, but determined to succeed, I dove into my mission.

As my battle began, a teasing breeze swept across the back-yard, sending all the little pieces of my puzzle flying playfully in the wind. Putting my fingers to my temples, I squinted my eyes, trying to recall every specification for what the Willy Wonka-Fun-Factory-Dreamland-Swing-Slide Fort was *supposed* to look like. The only part of the box that did *not* get blown away, was a torn triangular piece that had writing on it, which read, "Three hour assembly." *Three hours?* My man-mind instantly did the math, and I calculated that I could totally beat that time and be done in *one* hour! Convinced I was right, I gave the battle cry, "Let's do this thing!" The only one, who heard this declaration, was my dog, who seemed to be laughing at me.

Six to eight hours later, I hobbled around the ground, digging and raking-through the grass, trying to find the last bolt. I could not find it, but it did not matter. My fist gripped one of the support-beams, and I shook the set, to test its stability. It didn't move much and seemed sturdy enough. Just to make sure, I held the beam tightly and put my weight on it. This was not a good idea, as the whole set shifted back and forth. There was no way on earth *I* had missed *any* step in putting this thing together; so, I faulted the factory, for failing to include the missing bolt in the packaging, dismissing the structure's shifting as its being a fantastic feature of the play-set. It would be like a fun-house at the annual county fair.

I took a step away, to get a better view of my work of genius, and it was a bit unnerving. The fort's window was where the fort's floor was supposed to be; and there were large gaps between the ladder rungs and the monkey bars, that would require my children to have expert skills even Bear Grylls, from the show, "Man vs. Wild," doesn't even have. "It will be fine!" I muttered. Like a mountain-climber reaching his summit and planting his flag—sweat in my eyes, blood on my face, and dirt in my teeth—I raised my hands in victory and screamed the new name of the set, "Adventurous Wonder World!"

I looked at my children (who were crying), and I began to tear-up, believing they were overjoyed by the moment. (At least I kept telling myself this, as I nudged my sweet offspring toward the $400.00-purchase that promised hours of enjoyment.) As they reluctantly tip-toed a half-inch toward the swaying masterpiece, I heard from my boy five words that quickly altered my ego—"I'm not getting on that!" It was an EPIC FAIL! My kids can laugh about it now; but looking back, I should have followed the instructions.

Jesus is saying, when it comes to getting into Heaven, don't chunk His instructions and go at it your way. It doesn't work! You must follow God's plan! Otherwise, you don't make it. That was true two thousand years ago, and it's still true today. This may be simple to understand, in terms of the point Jesus is making, but it's quite difficult for people to comprehend, spiritually. That's why we need to take some time and watch our little video, slow it down, and pay attention to some details. Oh, by the way, don't think I have forgotten. I know you're still looking for the whole "GASP!"-connection. Hang in there; it's coming. Let's keep reading, because the gasp is at the core of the point Jesus is trying to make, here, in His outdoor church service among the olive trees.

Chapter Three

Report Cards

H it "Play" on the video. Do you see the faces of the crowd in the monitor of your mind? Press "Pause," and look at them. If facial expressions are a thermometer of the heart, then the now-cold stares coming from the crowd listening to Jesus, reveal their religious disapproval. Their wishes for an "everybody gets in" idea of Heaven have clashed with the teachings from the authoritative Rabbi. Hit "Play," again, and let's see what Jesus does next. Looks like He is going to just keep going with His sermon. Unmoved by the disgruntled gazes, Jesus slightly increases His volume and says, "Many will say to Me in that day, 'Lord, Lord, have we not prophesied in Your name, cast out demons in Your name, and done many wonders in Your name?'" — Stop, right there!

He mentions a particular day, but what day is He talking about? (It sounds pretty significant.) As curious as we may be about that day, the people within this gathering perfectly understand what day Jesus is speaking about. They know Jesus is talking about Judgment Day. The idea of a Judgment Day with God was not a foreign concept to these listeners. They grew-up being told about it, and they knew of their needing to be constantly ready for it. The Bible clearly points to the fact that one day all of humanity will undergo a Judgment Day with God. Scriptures are full of references to a day when God will judge the world. Psalms 96:13 says, "For He is coming, for He is coming to judge the earth." That's the day Jesus is speaking about, here, in His Sermon on the Mount. This same day was also mentioned in Acts 17:31 — "He has appointed a day on which He will judge the world."

Most people can't really catch the idea of what Judgment Day means. It's kind of hard for us to wrap our minds around it; but if you think about it, just like the culture, in which Jesus was speaking, it's not a foreign idea in our culture, either. There is something that lends insight to the idea of what Judgment Day is like—it's called a report card.

I remember my days, growing-up and going to public school in Florida. Throughout the school year, we were given a report card. Students still get these today, although the name of the card changes from state to state. Some call it a progress report, others refer to it as an education indicator, but the function is the same. It's a way to assess someone's comprehension skills and his overall behavior. I hated the days when I received my academic report card! The whole process was maddening. You go to school and take certain classes, such as math, science, and my personal favorite: physical education. Picture me, in 1980, with my toothpick-sized legs sticking out of a pair of Super-short, terrycloth, fuchsia-colored gym shorts; wearing high socks and a generic pair of sneakers. I got beat-up quite a bit for looking that way. (Moms and Dads?— Please, take a hint here: don't dress your kids in such a way that, when they get older and see a picture of themselves, it makes them want to come back home and slap you. Yes, I'm still in therapy over it. …Alas, I digressed; so let me get back to the report card.)

The document actually contained a listing of the classes I took. Next to each class was a symbol, usually a letter of the alphabet, indicating how well I did. I have *heard* that they gave out A's, B's, and C's for people who did well. (Although *I* never saw it, I *heard* about it.) However, I was well-aware of the fact that they gave out D's and F's for those who *thought* they were doing well, but their performances in the class suggested otherwise. –Is anybody feeling this with me, here? To top the whole grand experience off, you had to take the report card home to your parent or guardian, and have him or her review it. *Then*, you had to return the card *with a signature* on it, to prove that your authorities saw it. This, of course, meant there was *no* way I could avoid being grounded for-ev-errrrrrr! Oh, I loathed those days! I couldn't stand getting a report card. Giving an account of the way I conducted myself on my school campus, and suffering the consequences of my bad choices, was always a stressful and humiliating moment for me.

Perhaps it has been a while since you've had to endure the tension of getting a report card, but maybe it hasn't been that long since you've had to sit on the other side of an ominous desk at your job and undergo a performance-evaluation. (Those are quite the party, aren't they?) Your superior scrutinizes every functional objective you are responsible to perform, and how well you do on the evaluation, has everything to do with the way, in which you will get remunerated for the next year of your life. There is a lot at-stake during those evaluations. Undergoing such probes are intense and can leave you exhausted and stressed. But they dwarf in significance to the ultimate Performance Evaluation Day, the *supreme* Report Card Day that every human will face. Jesus calls it *"that day"*; it's when we will all stand before God to, not only give an account of the ways we conducted ourselves at school or handled the roles of our jobs, but we will also give an account of the ways we lived every waking-moment of our lives.

Ecclesiastes 12:14 sheds great light on this future day; it says, "For God will bring every work into judgment, including every secret thing, whether good or evil." That's pretty intense, isn't it? Oh, and it gets worse. Jesus went so far as to say that those things that we have done in secret will be revealed openly. In the Gospel of Luke 12:2-3, Jesus says, "For there is nothing covered that will not be revealed, nor hidden that will not be known. Therefore, whatever you have spoken in the dark will be heard in the light, and what you have spoken in the ear in the inner rooms will be proclaimed on the housetops." Put yourself there. You are face-to-face with the all-knowing God of the universe. God doesn't need a Smartphone to video your life; He has it all recorded in books. Revelation 20 tells us that on the Great White Throne Judgment Day, God will "open the books." Then, it's our turn to be in the place these folks in the first-century, heart-breaking story find themselves. There is not an experience on earth that will be able to compare to the nakedness and vulnerability we will feel in that moment.

You have got to be thinking that this is where the GASP!-point comes into focus, but it's not. It's coming, and this concept of judgment certainly should call all of us to be startled. But the GASP!-moment is far more intense, than a mere startling; it's exceedingly riveting and frightening! I need to back-off of that, though, for now. I can't go there, yet; but keep it on your radar, because it's coming. Right now, we are laser-focused on this *"day"* Jesus is talking about. It's one that we will all face. Hebrews 9:27 says, "And it is appointed for men to die once, but after that the judgment." One day we will all face this moment, and the people in the story Jesus is telling, are right, smack-dab in the middle of it. They are standing before their Maker on Judgment Day, and what happens to them, gives me great concern.

Chapter Four

Religious Swag

Hit "Play," again, on your mental-remote. —Whoa! You accidentally hit the "Fast-forward" -button at the same time. Jesus looked a little funny with His beard furiously flapping in the wind, and His arms waving up and down in fast-motion. (It felt a little irreverent hearing His voice at double-speed, making Him sound like one of the members of "Alvin and the Chipmunks." Well, as fun as it would be to play the whole thing in fast-forward, I'd better snap-out of my little ADD moment, and get serious.) Let's rewind to the scene, when Jesus was talking about people who were standing in judgment. —Hit "Stop!" That's it, right there. Now, go back just a *tiny* bit more to the frame, where the people who are facing judgment speak-up for themselves. Do you remember what they were saying to God? Let's catch it again. Hit "Play," and really listen this time. "Lord, Lord, have we not prophesied in Your name, cast out demons in Your name, and done many wonders in Your name?" —Pause it, right there! Now, let's break-down what we just heard.

(WOW! These folks had some serious religious-swag going on! All those spiritual activities would make a very impressive Facebook profile. Let's take a look at all the things they were pulling-off.) First, they claimed that they prophesied. This verb isn't talking about fore-telling the future, like the alleged-claims of psychics. They are not saying that they could somehow look into a crystal ball and predict what was going to happen in the future. This verb, "prophesied," means to forth tell, utter forth, or to declare. The context lends us to believe that what they would speak forth were things about God; and, according to their testimonies, they did it in His name. There-fore, we can conclude that these folks had a working-knowledge of God's revelation, and they had no trouble telling others about it.

They are much like many people around the world, who have exposed themselves to enough Bible, that they can tell others what God has to say about issues, such as marriage, homosexuality, and abortion. They can even quote a few of the Ten Commandments. These people in Christ's story could stand and declare God's take on big issues of life. This would put them in a position, where most ministry leaders would want to sign them up to be Bible study teachers. They seem to be among the top-of-the-class, for those whom we might call spiritual; and prophesying is just the first thing they mention in the grand list of their spiritual accomplishments.

On the heels of the great prophesying exclamation comes a bold testimony that they actually cast out demons! WOW! Did you notice the response of the crowd to this declaration? Jaws dropped and eyelids were flung wide open! These aren't your regular Sunday pew-warmers. These guys were engaged in serious spiritual warfare with Hell's thugs! [Demons are fallen angels, who were banished from Heaven, along with satan, when he tried to take over God's throne

(Isaiah 14:12-17; Ezekiel 28:11-19).] All throughout the Bible we see incidents, when people suffered from demon-possession.

In Mark chapter five, we read of a man from the country of the Gadarenes, who was demon-possessed. Jesus confronted the man, and when He did, the demons spoke-up and said that they were named Legion, because they were of a large number within the man. (Leading Christian band, Casting Crowns, wrote a chilling song about that story, called "Set Me Free.") The man's life was one of pain and isolation, as he cut himself often and lived in a graveyard. One encounter with Jesus, however, changed everything; the man was set free. This is the kind of warfare that these people, in the seventh chapter of Matthew, boasted of doing.

As the words, "We cast out demons in Your name," rolled-off the lips of Jesus, every ear in our tent perked-up, and the eyelids of the other hundreds of people flew skyward! These people were saying that they were full-on, front-line, spiritual-warfare specialists. (In the eyes of most folks, that makes them different from the rest of us church-goers--sort of like they're a kind of spiritual version of the U.S. Military's Special Ops--dubbed as "spiritually elite." I call them "casters." You won't find that term in the Bible, but it's what I call the people, who step-up to the plate and are willing to endure intense opposition—and even physical pain—when dealing with our spiritual enemy.)

Acts 19 records a story of a guy who tried to cast-out a demon. It mocked him, kicked his tail, and made him leave the fight, running home naked. Demon-casting is not for the faint-hearted. Jesus is saying that these guys, standing before Him on Judgment Day, are those that we Christian soldiers would call spiritually-elite Special Forces. That's quite a powerful skill! Knowing they also have spiritual revelation as prophesiers, puts these guys among the cream-of-the-crop.

The next thing out of their mouths gives their whole speech an infomercial-vibe. (Have you seen those mega advertisements? They promote a product, and after saying so many great things about it, an announcer interrupts the commercial and yells, "Wait, there's more!" That's the way this last statement comes across to me.) They say all these great things about themselves, and then they announce a tag-line, that seems to cover the whole gamut of every spiritual practice in the world. They declare that they have "done many wonders" in the name of God! (What wonders are they talking about? Like Criss Angel or David Blaine wonders?) Just exactly what do they mean?

The Greek word for "wonders" is *dynamis*. In this case, it's a feminine noun; it carries the idea of being a possession that's brought about by ability. Therefore, most translations of the Bible render the word "wonders" to mean works, which is to say these people do work for God. They aren't spiritual couch-potatoes. On the contrary, they are active in service for God.

Much like we have in the churches around the world today, people are quick to get involved and do something. They serve in the nursery, or show-up for a Saturday work-day. They are engaged in the Church family, teaching Sunday School classes, working in the parking-lot ministry, or serving at a men's wild-game dinner. We have people involved in all sorts of different works for God, and that's the kind of thing the people facing God's judgment in this story were involved in, as well. They were hard-working, religious people.

Man, what an amazing profile, containing Bible-drill winners, demon-slayers, and sweat-of-the-brow work-horses for God. For spiritually-elite people, such as these, you would think that God would shut-down the activity of Heaven; call for a full angelic choir to sing; get the celestial orchestra players to blast out the "Hallelujah Chorus," and welcome these people to Heaven, red-carpet style! But, that's not quite the response of God. In fact, His response is spiritu-ally terrifying!—The next words that come out of God's mouth are some of the most spiritually alarming words in all of Scripture.

Chapter Five

And Then

When the sun sets in the Middle East, it quickly gets cold. In our story's setting, the chill in the air is about to be invaded with some of the most fiery words these people have ever heard come out of a preacher's mouth. Reaching the end of His breath and intensifying His pace, Jesus says, "And then I will declare to them, 'I never knew you; depart from Me, you who practice lawlessness!'" Jesus concludes His message by putting together a powerful combination of eighteen words that construct the most spiritually-intense thoughts in Scripture. Don't miss this! Grab the remote, hit "Rewind," and let's slow-mo through these eighteen words.

These two words, *"and then,"* seem innocent and almost invisible; but remember, Jesus isn't the kind of teacher, who needs filler before He gets to the main point. It's all the main point to Him, and these two words are charged with purpose. To fully understand their meaning, just look at them in context. The people just finished speaking about their spirituality, and now, in response to what they said about their spiritual conditions, Jesus is about to speak some words to them. —Do you see it?

I am sure you are aware that it is very vogue to be spiritual these days. It's sort of trendy. As I travel the country, I get to speak to hundreds of thousands of people. When I ask them about their spirituality, everybody always has something to say about where they are, spiritually. Doctors, trash-collectors, students, and parents all have something to tell me. I'd bet that if I were there with you right now, even you would have something to say about your spiritual backstory. We all have something to say about our spiritual journeys, just like the people in the story Jesus is telling. When Jesus uses these two words, *"and then,"* He essentially says, "I've heard what you have said about your spiritual conditions, and it's My turn to speak and to say a word about it." Then, in eighteen simple words, He cuts through all the veneer of religious activity, unveiling the real conditions of their hearts.

I was watching CNN one day, and they did a very short, one-minute segment on the spirituality of America. Their research group discovered that over 80% of Americans say they are Christians. My first thought about that data was, "REALLY?" — America's morality has plummeted in the past decade. We have kicked the Ten Commandments out of the courthouses, banished prayer out of schools, and pimped porn like candy-corn to sugar-addicted kids! Everywhere I turn, another marriage is ending in divorce; and to top it off, illegal drugs are stupid-rampant. The list goes on and on, but I guess that's what happens in a country, where "80%" of those living in it, are "Christians." — Are you kidding me? Come on! Something isn't right. People can say all they want to CNN pollsters, but there is coming a day, just like in the lives of the people in Jesus' story, when people will be hushed by the holy gaze of God, and He will speak into the issues about their true spiritual conditions. Mark it down, there is coming an "and then" moment in a lot of people's lives.

In that moment, the text says that Jesus will declare something to them. The Greek tense of this phrase is future active indicative, bringing a sense of certainty to the claim. We don't have to guess; it's not that He *might*, or that He is simply "thinking about it"; or that He *could* reconsider. There is no mitigated speech here. He is making it clear that what He is about to say to these people can be etched into the granite of eternity, because He will never recant from making this statement. Which leads us, and all those listeners who encircled Him on the Mount of Olives that day, to lean-in to what He is about to say. (In the South, we have a little word we use to tell someone that it would be in his best interest to do something. We say, "It would behoove you…." Well, if I have ever told someone it would "behoove him" to do something, I'm doing it now, as it relates to paying attention to these last eleven words of Jesus.) His voice loud, yet soaked with heart-broken compassion, Jesus says, "I never knew you; depart from Me, you who practice lawlessness!"

Did you see it? Did you hear it? —You didn't? Then, let's rewind, and this time, think about what might be going on in the heads and hearts of the people, whom these words were directed toward. Think about it: these individuals are standing before God on Judgment Day, thinking that they are fine with God, and now they hear the worst eleven words a person could possibly hear in that moment: "I never knew you; depart from Me, you who practice lawlessness!" What do you imagine their responses would be, after hearing these terrible words? I'm thinking it might be something like,..."GASP!"

Yeah, a huge lung-expanding, heart-pounding, blood-pressure-raising, chest-grabbing, larynx-howling "GASP!" They are completely caught off-guard, and their minds are blown. They cannot believe what just happened to them. I call these people the most shocked people in all the Bible. Why do I think they are shocked? Because, I think that they thought they were in. I think they thought they had this Heaven-thing in-the-bag.

I would expect for you to question me on this. Having preached this message in arenas all over America, I've had many people who don't agree with me, when they first hear me say this. They bark, "Wait a minute, Preacher Tony. I understand using your imagination to make a point, but now you are taking a large leap and treading on conjecture." Perhaps, that's what you're thinking, too. If so, I understand, but answer this question. Who else, except someone who were certain of his salvation, would have the audacity to stand before God and pontificate such a spiritually-elite resume? Would you not agree, that only someone who believed that he were making it into Heaven, would dare do such a thing? That's who I think these people were; and now, their worst nightmares have become their eternal realities. They aren't going to Heaven, and they are shocked! ("GASP!"—It may be a terrific title for a book, but it's a terrifying end for a soul!) It's important to note that Jesus said this kind of thing is going to happen to *many* people. That concerns me, and it should also concern every other person, who cares about his own soul.

Earlier, I mentioned the CNN stats that reported 80% of people in the U.S. claim to be Christian. If you recall, I also stated that I thought those stats were wrong, based on the spiritual and moral inaptitude of our country. I actually think there is other information that more closely represents the spiritual condition of humanity, and it came from Dr. Billy Graham.

Dr. Graham is one of my heroes. Do a quick Google search, and you will discover that he is a hero to millions of other Christians around the world, as well. He is a champion among theological leaders. When one hears his simplistic Gospel messages, that have pointed millions to Jesus, it more than qualifies Dr. Graham as someone worth listening to and gleaning some insights from, about matters of spirituality.

In October of 2010, I was invited to visit Dr. Graham in his private home, nestled among the oaks, high atop a mountain in North Carolina. I was inspired by his small, simple house that he and his precious wife, Ruth, built. I was deeply moved by his humility and sincere desire for God to be glorified in all the achievements of his ministry. I don't think there was one sentence, in which he did not say, "Glory to God!" or "Praise Jesus!" It's in that same spirit—one that wants to honor God and to love people—that Billy once told the nation, during a Television broadcast, that he was burdened with the thought that over 75% of the people, who go to church or claim to be Christians, are actually lost and on their way to Hell.....*And they don't even know it.* He based this burden on the same verses that have been our focus here in this book: Matthew 7:21-23.

I'm not sure of the percentages, but I am certain of two things. First, by using the word "*many*," Jesus was warning us that it would be a large number of people. No matter how *many* the number is, it breaks down to individuals. That leads me to my second concern. To be one of those people, would have to be one of the most horrifying situations one would ever find himself facing. I would never want that to be me! *Jesus* doesn't want it to be *any* of us, and that's why He came...to warn us to be ready.

Chapter Six

News

I'd like to start this chapter with a question. But before the question, let's consider a few thoughts. When it comes to caring about their souls, most people do; but it's not really something we give great attention to. However, none of us would say that it's unimportant. Most people in the world would agree that it's *very* important. The millions of spiritual structures, chapels, synagogues, mosques, and churches sprawled across our globe, more than hint to the reality that humans care about their souls. So, my question presumes that you, along with billions of other people, care about the condition of *your* own soul.

Here's the question. Do you know *for certain* that this story Jesus is telling is not about you? Please, don't get upset with me here. I am not judging you. I'm asking, because I have a conviction, based on what I know about Scripture, that this *moment* that Jesus is speaking about, involves real people, who never saw it coming. I don't want this to be you, but no one else can answer for you, as to whether it is or not, *except* you.

I don't think most people get what's really going on between the lines of Matthew 7:21-23. Intellectually, I think we understand the words, but I don't think we quite grasp the weightiness, intensity, or the enormity of the dynamics going on, within the context of Christ's sermon. Sure, it was sunny; there was a large crowd; and Jesus was teaching about Judgment Day, but there was something supernaturally phenomenal going on beneath what, otherwise, might be seen as ordinary. I want us to see what that was, because there's a radical application to this phenomenon for you and me, personally. Our very souls will be eternally affected by it; therefore, we must not miss it! (It may sound wacky, but there's a television show that could shed some light on this for us.)

Have you ever seen the show, called *Early Edition*? It was an American television series that aired on CBS. Chances are, many of you have seen it. But in case you haven't, let me hook you up with a brief low-down. The show stars Kyle Chandler (who also starred in Spielberg's thriller, *Super 8*), playing the character, Gary Hobson. It was a pretty interesting show, set in Chicago, Illinois, detailing the adventures of a man and his mysterious happenings with the *Chicago Sun-Times*, which Gary receives from a ginger tabby-cat. —Yes, that's right, a cat delivers a newspaper to him every day at 6:30 a.m.

You know? —I can't resist injecting some good ol' cat-hater humor, right here. I'm thinking he should kill that cat. Yes, I did say kill. —Now, look what I've done! I just enraged cat-lovers every-where. You do know that cat lovers are a little on the serial side, don't you? Oh, yeah!—And there is a cat-lover, who just read those words, and it totally sent her over-the-edge.

You see, there are psychos, and then, there are cat-loving psychos. You don't want to anger either, but especially the cat-lovers. One of them probably just read this "kill the cat" statement, and at this very moment, she is rubbing her hands together—as villains do, when devising a sinister plan—and with her eyes wild with revenge and her grin devilishly wide, she says beneath her feline-loving breath, "Tony, you just said, 'Kill the cat!' I'm going to find out where you live, and put a bomb in your car."

My response to that is simple: Go ahead, put a bomb in my car—and I'll take the cat with me on a short drive!

—I don't do the cat-thing well, People! I'm of the persuasion that all dogs go to Heaven, and all cats go to, well,…you know. However, to keep from having to buy bomb-detection devices for my car, I think I should soften this up, a bit: He shouldn't kill the cat (hurts me to say that); but perhaps he should adopt it-out or put it in a shelter. Whatever he chooses to do, he should get rid of it. —Why? Not just because it's a cat (although that's reason enough); but because of the *kind* of newspaper it brings him every day. The newspaper is not a *normal* newspaper. It contained the news-of-the-day *before it actually happened*; hence, it was called the *Early Edition*. Usually, the headlines were something tragic, like "Five People Die in a Bank Robbery." Since Gary was made privy-to that information, he lived his life to intersect those moments, stopping the tragedies from occurring. As the television adventure unfolded, Gary successfully saved the day. When he did, the paper headlines changed from tragic—"Five People Die,"—to triumphant: "Bank Robbery Thwarted!" (Yay, Gary!)

I'd like to let you in on a little insider-info about the show.—Do I have your attention?—Okay, listen, the show?—It wasn't real. It was just a show. I know that may have some readers upset and screaming, "WHAT! Gary wasn't real? The cat was *fake*?" I'm sorry to have crushed you so deeply with this revelation, but you'll be okay. Just take a couple of deep breaths, join a yoga class, close your eyes, and chant, "I'm okay, it's okay; everything is going to be okay."

—Sarcastic, I know. You may be feeling like you want to join the Revenge for the Cats Club, that is after me, but I couldn't help myself here. I mean, come on! We all know it was simply a television show, and it *wasn't* real. Anybody in his right mind, knows that you can't possibly get the news about something *before* it *actually* happens. That's preposterous! ...Or is it? Oh, don't get me wrong. I'm not suggesting the show were real or even based on a real story. But now, I'm not talking about the show; rather, I'm referring to what was going-down on the sermon Jesus was preaching on that Middle Eastern hillside.

What I am trying to say, is that Jesus wasn't just teaching a simple sermon, for sermon's sake. He was authoritatively delivering news about a real event that is actually going to happen in the lives of real people! Matthew 7:21-23 is *God's Early Edition*! The all-knowing God of the universe is giving us a glimpse into the future. The headlines are tragic: "Good Person, Loved by Friends and Family, Doesn't Make It into Heaven." Now, in a phenomenon of supernatural revelation, Jesus fast-forwards into the future, sees this moment happening, and reports it back to those in the present. Can you see how that foreknowledge of truth makes this story so powerful? Since that is the back-story of these verses, can you understand what makes them so personally important to every human being?

Why did Jesus tell a story about this future moment that people were going to have with God on Judgment Day? What was His purpose for sharing this type of *Early Edition*? Was Jesus just wanting to rub-it-in? Many of the people standing there while He preached, were going to be the same folks, who would later shout for Pilate to crucify Him. Therefore, was His heart revengeful, and He was just letting them have it? Was He just declaring that their "day of reckoning" would come? Or could it be, because 2 Peter 3:9 tells us that God "is long-suffering toward us, not willing that any should perish, but that all should come to repentance," that He was sharing this news, to give them the chance to do something about it? I believe, out of His great love for them—and for us—He delivered this *Early Edition*, to warn people, so that we might change our current, devastating headlines of our life stories—"Going to Hell"—to a full-page, bold-print, delightful one: "Going to Heaven!"

My heart tells me that Jesus' motive and message were to warn us. When I look at the whole life of Jesus, it clearly communicates that His intent was to *save*, not to slam. He is giving us this insight, so that we will be ready to meet Him on Judgment Day.

Chapter Seven

Don't Scoff

I think it's imperative that we really comprehend what the whole concept of a *devastating headline* involves. These people are experiencing the end of their lives, as they've known it; and they are entering into eternity. What really gets me about this story is that we will all face this sort of moment one day, and what stirs my heart is that we don't know when, or even how, it will happen.

One of the ways this day could come is by, what many call, the "end of the world." Do you remember what the Bible said in 2 Peter 3:9? (I quoted it earlier, about God not wanting any person to perish.) If you keep reading through that chapter of 2 Peter, it deals with some alarming apocalyptic themes. (Peter's words remind me of a haunting Johnny Cash premonition-song, called, "When the Man Comes Around." It will raise the hairs on the back on your neck!) 2 Peter 3:10-12 puts it like this: "But the day of the Lord will come as a thief in the night, in which the Heavens will pass away with a great noise, and the elements will melt with a fervent heat; both the earth and the works that are in it will be burned up. Therefore, since all these things will be dissolved, what manner of persons ought you to be in holy conduct and godliness, looking for and hastening the coming of the day of God, because of which the Heavens will be dissolved, being on fire, and the elements will melt with fervent heat?"

If there has ever been an intense section of Scripture in the Bible, there it is! Peter says the end of the world will come, and when it does, all of humanity will stand before God for judgment. However, there are many people, who blow-off the whole idea of the "end of the world." The thought gets dismissed from their radars, because people have been saying that it will happen for decades. Yet, it still hasn't happened. —I can understand that, but I would caution all of us to take a little life-lesson from the people, who were guilty of doing the same thing in the days of Noah.

Peter gives us the same admonition in verse four, when he mentions scoffers: people, who blow-off warnings about the end of the world, by saying, "Where is the promise of His coming? Our ancestors who have fallen asleep [died] said this their whole lives, and so did their ancestors before them, but it still has yet to happen." Peter responds to this skepticism by pointing back to the era of the flood. He is inviting the readers of his letter to learn from one of the most tragic global disasters in world history.

We all should take a moment to think about the plight of these people. Jesus thought we should, as well, because He also made a statement that paralleled the flood of Noah's day, to the end of the world described in Peter's letter. Answering His disciples, who were asking when this end would come, Jesus says in Matthew 24:36-39, "But of that day and hour no one knows, not even the angels of heaven, but My Father only. But as the days of Noah were, so also will the coming of the Son of Man be. For as in the days before the flood, they were eating and drinking, marrying and giving in mar-riage, until the day that Noah entered the ark, and did not know until the flood came and took them all away, so also will the coming of the Son of Man be."

By now, you know how my imagination works. When I hear Jesus say this, it's like my mind goes into movie-mode, and I see the whole event unfolding, as it happened. It's horrible! 2 Peter 2:5 tells us that Noah was a preacher of righteousness. He preached that man was sinful and needed to be right with God. Then, he preached even louder with his hammers and saws, through the construction of a massive ark. The message was clear: we are sinful, and God is going to judge us.

The ark was safety from the coming wrath, but sadly, we have no account of anyone else on the earth, who got into the ark, other than Noah's family of eight. It could just be that everybody else scoffed, thinking that Noah was just some sort of religious zealot. Can't you see them mocking the "freak," who was building the big boat, while he preached about a day when it was going to rain, and a flood was going to wipe everything out? It's not hard to imagine their dismissing it (and him) as nonsense, but I'd caution you not to join them.

Imagine families that traveled that part of the earth, strolling by, and seeing the super- sized boat almost at its completion. Perhaps a daddy with his wife and two children were there. His little girl clutches his hand and asked, "Dad, do you think there is really going to be a flood?" To which the dad may have replied, "Honey, they have been saying this as long as I can remember." As he points to a tree, he tries to comfort her. "See the carving in that tree? That's your grandfather's initials, and those are mine beside them. He took me here when I was a kid, his father took him, and we've been hearing about this all our lives, and it hasn't happened. "Don't worry, Honey; everything is as it should be." She smiles in approval, and they walk off.

Now, fast-forward a few years. Go there with me in your mind. Do you see the little town on the outskirts of the place where Noah was building the boat? It's dusk and everyone is getting ready to eat dinner and retire for the evening. Do you see the little warm, cozy, clay house, there, in the middle of the town? It has a flickering oil lamp sitting on the ledge of the window. Do you see the worn and weathered, wooden door? Gently push it open, and step inside.

The tiny house is even smaller on the inside, isn't it? It's only one open room, divided into four quarters. On the far left, you see the bed pads made of sheep's wool, and the other end of the room is a place for the storage of dry-goods and clothing. Look to your right, and you will notice the room is divided into a dining area and a very crude kitchen. The wall of the kitchen is discolored with soot from the fireplace and stove combination. There are only a few bowls and pots, and the dining area has an ankle-high round table, where the family members recline each night, to relax and eat their humble dinner.

Do you see the little boy and girl at the table? She's got a butterfly in her wool head scarf, and her little brother is hiding a lizard beneath his tunic. As he stares at the butterfly, he is working up a plan to make sure his lizard gets to eat dinner, too. His sister notices and screams, and her little brother shouts back at her. As Dad blasts through the door, the yelling instantly halts. He's hungry and muttering beneath his breath about a wolf he chased off, while shepherding, earlier that day. Mother comes to the table with a plate of fish and herbs. The children start telling-on each other at the same time, and Mom delightfully brags about the money she saved, purchasing the fish at the market today. The chatter continues, as they dig-in and start eating. —Do you see it? It's a harmoniously domestic moment.

Without warning, the Norman-Rockwell scene is abruptly interrupted, as thunder rolls and shakes every house in town. The dad jumps-up from the table, racing to discover what caused the quaking. He swings the front door open, and his fears escalate, as he sees lightning cut across the ominously dark sky. His children grip his legs, screaming to know what is going on. His wife says nothing with her lips, for fear of further-scaring the children; but her eyes have a thousand questions. The thunder explodes around them, rattling the wooden plates on the table. A torrential downpour begins to soak their surroundings, extinguishing the lamp in the window.

Little dark spots pepper the father's light-blue cloak, as the wind violently whisks the rain through the doorway, where he stands. The sky, billowing with a cataclysmic fury of blackish-purple clouds, unleashes larger, heavier raindrops. Then, in a horrifying moment of recollection, the father remembers Noah, the "ark-constructing freak," and his message. Flashes of bright, white light reflects off the faces of his children; scooping up his children, he screams to his wife, as they run to the ark for safety.

But, when he gets there, it's too late. God closed the door to this massive boat. As the torrential waters rise, the daddy beats on that ark to no avail, until blood gushes from his fists. Then, helplessly, he watches his boy slip under the water. Another violent wave crashes over them, and his little girl is swept away. Screaming, his wife chokes on the muddy water, and within seconds, the undertow sucks her to the bottom. The man now has his fingernails clawing into the gopher wood panels of the boat, giving every last ounce of energy to hold himself up, until he loses his grip, plummeting knee-over-head into the watery grave. As his lungs fill with the gritty-brown flood waters, his fists shake toward the heavens. He can't blame God for this disaster that has come upon him, because God—being great in mercy and grace—provided a way to escape. He had warned the man his entire life that this day was coming. How tragic that he failed to listen!

God promised He wouldn't flood the whole earth again with water. It's true, He won't; but another kind of flood is coming, and this one will be with fire. Peter, inspired by the Holy Spirit, said, "The heavens will pass away with a great noise, and the elements will melt with a fervent heat; both the earth and the works that are in it will be burned-up. "...The heavens will be dissolved, being on fire, and the elements will melt with fervent heat." Jesus said the end will come. In that time, people will be preoccupied with living for their own interests, their goals, ambitions, and their self-absorbed affections. And in an instant, the end will come! Just like in the days of Noah—but this time, with fire. When I read those words penned by Peter, I want to make sure I am ready for that day, and I have a passion to make sure others are ready, as well.

I think it may be appropriate to invite you to take a moment and exhale, before we go into the next chapter. This is intense stuff, dealing with a serious matter, and is emotionally difficult to swallow. Take a breather for a minute; close your eyes. Ask God to keep speaking to your heart and to help you open your mind and spirit to fully-comprehend this *Early Edition* that He preached long ago, on that rolling hillside in east Jerusalem. He preached it with such passion, because He knows the end will come for you one day, and He *wants* you to be ready.

Chapter Eight

Be Prepared

It's completely understandable how people can brush-off the idea that one day the whole world will end. It hasn't happened since the flood; therefore, they think it won't happen at all. I get it; however, when it does come, God won't be considerate of their opinions. The *end* will obliterate them, in an instant. I believe the day will happen, but I certainly understand the logic that causes people to dismiss the whole idea. There is, however, another way that life could change forever, and to deny that this day could happen, is inexcusable. The moment is called Death.

Death has an impressive track record. The statistics for death are amazing; every one out of one person dies. I don't have to spend a large amount of time convincing you that death is real. We all have loved ones, who have passed away. I sat down one day and wrote a list of people that I have known who have died; it was an emotionally-exhausting exercise. The list got so large I couldn't do it anymore. Don't worry, I'm not going to ask you to create a list. We don't need to make a list to realize death is real. There are other things that remind us of death's reality.

I'm certain there is a cemetery close to your home. I have one close to where I live, and every time I pass by it, I am reminded about the certainty of death. No one argues with the fact that death is real. The Bible is very clear about the certainty of death for every person. Psalm 104:29 says, "You [God] hide Your face, they are troubled; You take away their breath, they die and return to the dust." This verse is one that has inspired ministers, who officiate funerals, to indisputably say, "From ashes to ashes, and from dust to dust." We are all destined for the grave. When I hear these words, there is a little voice in the back of my head telling me that it's all true. Perhaps you've heard that voice, as well. It's an indisputable fact that we will all die one day, but I've discovered an interesting struggle with denial that happens when I think of death.

Fueled by my tenacious desire to live, the volume of this voice gets louder. I find myself suppressing any thoughts of leaving my loved ones, not reaching my life's goals, or departing with so many unfulfilled dreams. I've talked with many other people, who have experienced this same exhausting, internal war. Nonetheless, struggle as we might, we can't deny that death will happen. Ecclesiastes 9:5 says, "For the living know that they will die." We all know it's real. We don't need to attend a debate to hear Team Life spar with Team Death. We are convinced it is real, and there is no escaping it. As a matter of fact, I bet what's true about my family is true about your family, too; death runs in my family. Think about it. It's real, and it is coming for us all…and most people never see it coming.

The hard drive of my mind is filled with sad files about the subject of death that I'd rather not open. Some are about my own family members, others are personal friends; but the majority are stories

I've gotten through phone calls, Tweets, Facebook posts, or emails. All of them move me, but there is one that stands out, as I write this chapter.

It happened on an evening after I preached to a capacity-crowd, in the Sun Dome Arena, in Tampa, Florida. We experienced a supernatural movement of God that night, as over two thousand people made professions of faith in Jesus Christ. Sometime after the concert was over, we got a tragic report that three students, who attended the event, were killed in an automobile accident. Our hearts were broken, and we hurt deeply for the families having to live with the fall-out of such devastating losses. I have met the family members of each of these teenagers, and although the families were crushed emotionally, they were comforted by the assurance that their children were with God in Heaven. One mother even quoted 2 Corinthians 5:8, which says, "We are confident, yes, well pleased rather, to be absent from the body and to be present with the Lord."

A staggering detail of this story is that one of the students, only two hours earlier, had repented and trusted Christ for salvation, during the invitation I extended at the end of my message. WOW! With only a hundred and twenty minutes left to live, a young sixteen-year-old responded by faith to the Gospel. In his book, <u>i am not, but i know I AM</u>, Louie Giglio nailed it, when he wrote, "Life is brief and our time on earth is short." Whether you have a hundred and twenty minutes left to live, or seventy years, James 4:14 says, "For what is your life? It is even a vapor that appears for a little time, and then vanishes away." Death comes for us all.

There are those who, knowing death is coming, live to get all they can out of life, with no thought to their futures. However, in Isaiah 22:13, God warns against espousing a mantra that says, "Let us eat and drink, for tomorrow we die!" That's not to say, God doesn't want us to enjoy life. Although the Bible clearly warns against indulging the flesh, it also invites us to experience pleasure. Ecclesiastes 5:17-18 says, "Here is what I have seen: It is good and fitting for one to eat and drink, and to enjoy the good of all his labor in which he toils under the sun all the days of his life which God gives him." God wants us all to enjoy life, but not at the expense of being unprepared for death! Did you get what you just read in that last sentence? So you don't miss it, I want to repeat a part of it that deserves your attention: enjoy life, but not at the expense of being unprepared for death.

All this talk about death is probably bringing you down. I understand. Nobody likes the subject. Research teams have discovered that death is the number-one fear of most people in the world. (Well, except for comedian Chris Rock, who said, when he was asked about fearing death—"I am not afraid of death; I just don't want to be there when it happens." I think we could all say a LOL, amen to that!) Most people would love to have some sort of way to cheat death. Some people get extensions on life through surgeries and medical treatments, but those services do not provide any chances to bypass death. That fact, alone, should propel all of us to make sure we are ready for it.

One of my favorite animated movies of all time is called "Hoodwinked." It's the kind of movie, in which there are so many interrelated moments in the film that describing any scene could ruin it for you. It's amazing, but there is one part of the film that keeps repeating itself in my head, in view of this chapter on death. (If you haven't seen the movie, it's still safe to keep reading. I will make sure there's no spoiler here.) One of the characters is a goat that lives on top of a mountain (as he should), and he sings, instead of speaks. A witch puts a spell on him, and now he can't talk; instead, he has to sing everything he wants to say, and his singing is quite an awful sound (think bleating-goat, mingled with Willie Nelson).

The other interesting thing about this goat is that he has inter-changeable horns. He has a whole house-full of them, and he switches them out, based on whatever he needs. He has some that open pickle jars, others that are used for TV reception, and even a set that serves as helicopter blades. As he shows you all his horns for every occasion, he tells you all about them in a song. The song is called, "Be prepared!" (My daughter can sing every word of it and can sound just like him. She says it's a gift from God, but I'm thinking she shouldn't blame Him for it.) There is one line in the little ditty that stands out to me; it says, "Be prepared, be prepared;

this lesson must be shared. Be prepared, be prepared; and unless you got a spare, you got one life, so handle it with care!" Every time I hear that little song, I am reminded that we don't have a "spare life." And when it comes to death, we had *better* be prepared.

Hebrews 9:27 gives us insight as to why we should be prepared for death—"And as it is appointed for men to die once, but after this the judgment." When life on earth has ended, we will face God in judgment. I talked about that moment, earlier, in chapter three. The Big Report Card is coming for us, after we die. We only have the time while we are alive, to get ready for that big moment. After we die, it's too late to do anything about it. What happens to us after judgment, is eternal.

Chapter Nine

Forever Somewhere

Let's get back to the video on my Smartphone. I am going to rewind back to that moment, when the individuals are gasping, after hearing Jesus say, "Depart from Me." It's quite clear that these people, although quite religious, were not prepared for their Judgment Day. Does your mind race with questions about what is going to happen to them, now that they aren't going to Heaven? Mine does.

I operate from a deep conviction, believing everybody will spend forever somewhere, and there are only two options: Heaven or Hell. Jesus just told these folks to leave His presence, and this can only mean one thing: they are not going to Heaven, which means they are going to Hell. At this news from Jesus, their knees buckle, perspiration beads their upper lips, and their eyes glaze-over in disbelief. Wouldn't the same be happening to you and me, if that were you and I? —Could anything be more tragic, than that sort of headline summing-up our stories, on the front-page of the *Eternal Times*? Like I said earlier, their worst nightmares have now become their eternal realities.

Hell is a very touchy subject these days. It's not met with much approval, even among churches. Be that as it may, no matter how much the theological tides may ebb on this subject, it's a reality that Jesus taught. In Matthew 5:22, Jesus said there are those, who are in "danger of hell fire." Later, in the account of Matthew 13, Jesus talks about people, who will be cast "into the furnace of fire, where there will be wailing and gnashing of teeth." In Luke 12:5, Jesus tells us to fear the One, Who has the "power to cast into Hell." What is so terrifying about Hell? What is there to fear about being cast into this place?

In the book of Revelation, we see Hell described in two words. Revelation 21:8 says, "But the cowardly, unbelieving, abominable, murderers, sexually immoral, sorcerers, idolaters, and all liars shall have their part in the lake which burns with fire and brimstone, which is the second death." Did you see them? The two words are "second death." This is mind-blowing stuff. You die once on the earth; and if you go to Hell, you die forever. Heaven is referred to as a place of everlasting life. Hell, on the other hand, is called the "second death," which is to say it's a place of everlasting death. Those who go to Hell will experience, for all of eternity, the thing that people fear the most: death.

Being a minister, I am often engaged in conversations that deal with the subject of death. There are many who have confided in me about their fears of death. There are multiple reasons we have for fearing death, but when you break it down, it's interesting to discover that the thing many people fear most about death is the way that they are going to die. If you give people a choice of dying a slow, very painful, long, drawn-out death; or a quick, instant, get-it-over-with death, one hundred percent of the people I have spoken with, pick "instant." Nobody wants it to be painful and drawn-out. I need you to really lean-in to what I am about to say to you in this moment. Do you understand that since Hell is called the second death, that means people will be stuck in a state of dying that never ends, and do you know the way they will be dying? They will be burning to death. How horrific!

Along with the other verses we have already looked at, Jesus described Hell in vivid detail. It's important to understand that He didn't do so, in order to scare us; but rather, He was trying to warn us. He was giving us an *Early Edition.* In the Gospel account of Luke 16, Jesus gives us insights about Hell that are staggering to the human mind. In verses nineteen through twenty-six, Jesus gives us a view into the horrors of Hell. He said, "There was a certain rich man, who was clothed in purple and fine linen, and fared sump-tuously everyday. On the other hand, there was a certain beggar, named Lazarus, full of sores, who was laid at his gate, desiring to be fed with the crumbs which fell from the rich man's table. Moreover, the dogs came and licked his sores. So it was, that the beggar died, and was carried by the angels to Abraham's bosom. The rich man also died, and was buried. And being in torments in Hades, he lifted up his eyes and saw Abraham afar off, and Lazarus in his bosom. Then, he cried and said, 'Father Abraham, have mercy on me, and send Lazarus that he may dip the tip of his finger in water and cool my tongue; for I am tormented in this flame.' But Abraham said, 'Son, remember that in your lifetime you received your good things, and likewise Lazarus evil things; but now he is comforted and you are tormented. And besides all this, between us and you there is a great gulf fixed, so that those who want to pass from here to you cannot, nor can those from there pass to us.'"

It's important to note that Hades is Hell. There are many theologians, who debate as to whether the two places are the same, but once one sees what this man has to endure, it's easy to conclude that he is in Hell. This story rocks me to my core! My gut wrenches, thinking about what the man in Hell is experiencing. First of all, he is remembering the times. Abraham says, "Remember in your lifetime." Hell is a place, where people are haunted with the perpetual memory of better days, and perhaps opportunities forfeited to change their eternal conditions. They are anguished with regret that they wasted their precious and limited time on earth, feasting on the temporal things and neglecting to prepare for eternity.

He is also reach-less and trapped. In that Scripture passage, Jesus said, "…There is a great gulf fixed." There is a permanent chasm separating Heaven and Hell. It's there, keeping anyone in Heaven from being able to reach out and save those in Hell, "so that those who want to pass from here to you cannot." This is one reason we should do all we can to reach people with the Gospel now. It's one of the reasons the person, who gave you this book took a risk of causing stress in your relationship. He or she knows we can't do anything to help you, once you die.

The gap also serves as a barrier, forbidding escape for all who go there — "nor can those from there pass to us." In America, we have an emergency-rescue system, whereby someone can use a phone, dial 9-1-1, and help will be on the way. In Hell, there is no 9-1-1. You are reach-less and trapped! Still, the most frightening thing we see about this peek into Hell, is that this man is a recipient of torments. Hell's fury has many inflictions, but the one we see here, that dwarfs all other pains, is fire. The man exclaims that he is "tormented in this flame." I cannot even begin to imagine a more terrifying existence.

I've had doctors tell me that there is nothing more painful, than to be severely burned. I recall an event, early in my Christian life that marked me. A teenager was smoking a cigarette one day, while pumping fuel in his vehicle. His carelessness caused a huge explosion, and the boy was burnt to the bone. I had friends that visited him in the hospital. What they described, after visiting with him, is unnerving, and it pushes my emotions to the point of despair over the thought of anyone who goes to Hell.

The student was a white young man, but he was so severely burned, that his arms were charred-black all the way through. The doctors were careful not to touch his fingers, for fear that they might snap-off. One friend who went to the hospital to minster to the boy, said what he saw was so terrible, that nothing in his ministry training ever prepared him for it. When he entered into the emergency room, the boy looked like a blob of violently convulsing, melted flesh. The minister approached the student to pray over him. He remarked that he was rushing to get out of the room, because the stench of burning flesh was so nauseating. As he went to pray, he looked into the boy's disfigured melted face. His eyes were bulging from his skull, and he seemed to be reaching for help, like the hands of a person drowning and grasping for rescue. Then came the noise, sounding like a gurgling-hiss. He was desperately trying to say something to the preacher. At first, my friend could not make out what the boy was saying. After a few attempts, it became clear what was being said. With blistered lungs and scorched lips, the boy began crying in a low hoarse groan, "Kill me! Kill me! Kill me!"

I'll never forget the day I heard this story. Could you imagine being that boy? Can you imagine being in that condition for all eternity? That's the fate of all who go to Hell. They will be stuck in a state of dying that never ends, and the way they will be dying is by burning to death.

As I write this story, my eyes swell with tears. My throat tightens, and my bottom lip quivers, for my heart is breaking. I don't like to talk about Hell. With all the baggage of my past, I really don't like to talk about stuff that causes emotional turmoil and spurs rejection. I would rather extend an olive branch and an invitation to serenity. The subject of Hell tempts me to wave the white flag of surrender and sign a peace-treaty that could usher a whole new era, where everyone would make it to tranquil ground. Nevertheless, if I really care about your soul, I have to risk being misunderstood and to bear the emotional tension. I am willing to do that, because I really believe that everybody will spend forever somewhere, and I don't want it to be Hell; I want it to be Heaven. The incredible thing is that God wants this for you—*even more than I do*!

Chapter Ten

Believe

As I've preached across America in stadiums, arenas, and churches, I've discovered that the subject of Hell gets people emotionally-charged. I've receive hundreds of emails from disgruntled people, who have heard me touch on Hell in my Gospel presentations. They say things like, "God is a mean God, because He sends people to Hell." I don't see it that way. What I read in New Testament Scriptures leads me to believe that God doesn't send anyone to Hell. Rather, one chooses to crawl into Hell over God's dead, yet resurrected body: the Lord Jesus Christ. The Bible says in John 3:16, "For God so loved the world that He gave His only begotten Son, that whosoever believes in Him should not perish but have everlasting life." Do you see it? That one verse tells us that God, in a great act of love, gave His Son, Jesus, much like He gave the ark before the flood. He did this, so that people could be saved from His wrath. God is good like that. He is far from being a mean God. If someone goes to Hell, it's because he chose to reject God's way of escape or rescue.

Matthew 25:41 takes it a step farther and tells us that Hell wasn't even made for humans. It was "prepared for the devil and his angels." God doesn't want you, or anyone else, tormented in Hell. He designed Hell to be a place of banishment for satan and his demons. God desires for you to be saved. His heart is that you would receive this spiritual *Early Edition* and experience a life-change, so that you spend forever with Him. When I read Matthew 7:21-23, I can feel God's redemptive compassion in each word that rolled-off the caring lips of Jesus. Christ's heart was breaking for those people. He knows what fate could await those listening to Him, and His desire is that each one of them would be saved, and not shocked. What's more is that He has this same desire for both you and me. What happens to those people in the story Christ gave us in Matthew, is tragic. There are going to be many people who have to suffer in Hell forever, and just as He didn't want this fate for any of those people listening to Him, as He preached the Sermon on the Mount, He doesn't want it for you, either.

My mind wonders how the people responded to what He had to say that day. Apart from calculating the number of sheep he was entrusted to watch, I'm curious as to what the local shepherd thought? If I could read minds, what would I hear drifting through the thoughts of the lady I almost knocked-over, earlier, under our tent? What was racing through the over-active mind of a tax collector's teenage son, who had been going to the synagogue, since he was a baby? Actually, I'm equally interested in what *your* response is to the story Jesus is telling? This brings us back to the question that I asked earlier: do you know His story is not about you? Do you know that this *Early Edition* is not the story of how your life has to end and your eternity begins? Do you know that you are one-hundred-percent-prepared for your day of judgment? The nature of these questions, spurs all of us to take them seriously.

I can't tell you if Matthew 7:21-23 is about you. I have no way of knowing that, but one thing I do know is this: I have yet to meet anyone, who wants this story to be about him! Most people I meet, want to make sure they don't miss Heaven; and, chances are, you feel the same way. If that is the case, then let me tell you how you can make sure it's not about you. It's actually sort of simple, really. Here is the key (--just make sure you don't miss it, the way they missed it!): every sweating human being standing in the sun, soaking-up Jesus' words that day, clearly understood that the people in the story were not going to Heaven. They missed it! It won't be a big mystery to everyone else, who reads this book, as to where these people ended-up after the judgment. They missed Heaven, and they went to Hell. They *missed* it, and we just need to make sure that *we* don't miss it, the same way they did. I think they fundamentally missed it, by having an improper belief in Jesus; their issue simply involved this component: what does it *really* mean to believe in Jesus?

John 3:16 says that those, who "believe," are the ones, who get everlasting life, as opposed to everlasting death. John 1:12 says, "To them He gave the right to become children of God, to those who believe in His name." In John 11:25, Jesus said, "I am the resurrection and the life. He who believes in Me, though he may die, he shall live." It's clear that believing is the key to obtaining everlasting life. Believing is the icon that we need to click and drag the mouse of our hearts on, in order to obtain eternal access in Heaven. Since this is the case, it's crucial that we have a full understanding as to what it means to correctly believe in Jesus.

Let's do a little experiment together that might prove to be helpful in getting a handle on what it means to properly believe in Jesus. I'm going to quote a couple of verses from the Bible, and I want you to pay close attention to the theme of belief, threaded throughout these verses. Let's look at Romans 10:9-10, which says, "If you confess with your mouth the Lord Jesus, and believe in your head that God has raised Him from the dead, you will be saved. For with the head one believes unto righteousness, and with the mouth confession is made unto salvation." Did you dial-in on what was being said in those verses? If you didn't, I need to let you in on a little something. I didn't quote those verses correctly; I changed something in them. Let's see if you can detect what was changed. I will write them again, and this time, I will write them the way they actually appear in the Bible. "If you confess with your mouth the Lord Jesus, and believe in your heart that God has raised Him from the dead, you will be saved. For with the heart one believes unto righteousness, and with the mouth confession is made unto salvation."

Take a minute and compare the accurate verses with the first ones I wrote. Go back and look at them carefully. Did you notice anything different between the two? I'm sure you did. The difference deals with the words, "head" and "heart." I used "head" in my first rendering, and it actually says "heart," in the Bible. You caught that, didn't you? Intellectually, it would be hard for anyone to miss that, but here is the kicker: Jesus said many people will miss it spiritually. The "many" that are mentioned in Matthew 7 have missed

Heaven and are going to Hell, because they had a belief about Jesus in their heads, but not in their hearts. If you want to make sure you don't end up like they did, you must make sure you believe the Gospel *in your heart.*

According to the Bible, believing is the core connection-point, to gaining access to Heaven. It's important to make sure we have this issue covered correctly. We need to make sure our belief is not just in our heads, but in our hearts, as well. But how can we do inventory in these places, to make sure we've got this belief-issue covered correctly? Our anatomies are not designed to be able to just take a peek inside our heads and hearts, to see if we have any belief in there. We weren't born with little latches on our foreheads or chests. (That would make it easy, wouldn't it? Just stand in front of a mirror, turn the latch; pry open the small door, and take a peek around, to make sure belief is nestled in its rightful place.) With such an immense importance attached to whether or not we believe in Jesus in our hearts, it's crucial to be certain that we've done so. But without the "latches," how can we determine the states of our beliefs? Perhaps a story about a waterfall and a tightrope-walker could help us in this

matter of knowing whether or not we have authentically believed in

our hearts.

Chapter Eleven

Really Believe

In June of 1859, Jean Francois Gravelet stretched a tightrope across the Niagara Falls. Almost everyone in America is familiar with this great icon of tourism. It's a massive waterfall, dumping 1,590,000 gallons of water per second over its edge. That's raging water! Gravelet, who also went by the stage name of "The Great Blondin," had a rope secured 130 feet above the raging water and stretched 330 feet across. Then, he announced that he would walk across Niagara Falls on the thin rope.

Thousands of people showed up to watch, and as He was about to begin his spectacular feat, he looked out at the gathered masses and asked them to get him a wheelbarrow. A low male voice came from the crowd, "What for?" A different high-pitched voice followed, "We don't know." A raspy, old, male voice chimed-in, "Sometimes these guys use umbrellas, other times they use bicycles, and many of them use big poles. We don't care, get the guy a wheelbarrow. We just want to see him fall!" Laughter permeated amongst the group of spectators, and in a few minutes, Blondin had his wheelbarrow. With his hands gripped on the handles, he rolled the bucket on its one wheel all the way across the massive waterfall.

Once he made it to the other side, the crowd burst into applause. Instantly, the high-flying enthusiast turned around, and he walked all the way back across the tightrope! As he arrived successfully to a safe place, the crowd went into a frenzy of amazement! Then, to their utter astonishment, the Great Blondin started to cross again for the third time. He was about to take his first step, when he looked out at the crowd and paused to ask them a simple question.

The crowd members' necks were stretched upward, and their eyes were squinted beneath the tiny shade provided by the saluted posture of their hands across their eyebrows. Blondin let them stare a few seconds longer, clutching another moment of dramatic effect. Then, he asked, "Do you guys believe I can do it again?" With a roar, the people instantly replied, "Yes!" They had just watched him do it twice. Their minds calculated his skills, times the length, plus the success rate, and it all added up to the fact that he was completely capable. So their volume increased, and they kept chanting, "Yes! Yes! Yes!" Blondin waved his hands, as to invite the crowd to quiet down, but they kept cheering, "YES! We believe! We believe!" He intensified the waving movement with his hands, and incrementally the huge throng started to hush. In a domino effect, silence began to fall over the crowd from the front to the back.

Satisfied that they could all hear him now, Gravelet scanned the faces of those who had gathered to watch his death-defying feat. Moments earlier, they were screaming that they believed he could do it, and now they stood silent, inquisitive about his next step. He stuck out his arm and pointed his finger at the left side of the crowd, slowly moving it to the right side, and with a loud voice, he probed, "Okay, then, the person, who really believes, get in the wheelbarrow!" By now, his hands were directed at the wheelbarrow, fingers extended, palms up, welcoming any takers. The silence deepened. No clapping, no cheering, just the sound of the falls churning in the background. His words, like the falls, were tumbling through their minds, "Get in the wheelbarrow." His invitation was a fork-in-the-road, as each individual was now challenged to make the conduct of their lives match the claims of their lips. If they really believed, they would have to prove it.

Did you know that when it comes to believing in Jesus, He is asking no less of you and me? We are transgressors against the Law of God; and, consequently, we will stand in judgment one day. Romans 3:23 says, "We all have sinned and fallen short of the glory of God." We are all sinners. I've never met anyone who hasn't broken one of the Ten Commandments of God. I'm certain you have your share of sins, just as I do! Romans 6:23 says, "The wages of sin is death." Because of our sins, we are in danger of being tormented in Hell forever. But the rest of Romans 3:23 says, "...The gift of God is eternal life, through Jesus Christ our Lord." Jesus came to earth, lived a sinless life, went to the Cross, and died to take our punishment for our sins. Three days later, He rose from the dead. And now, at this very moment, He's in heaven, at the right hand of God the Father. Jesus stands in the gap between us and the coming force of the wrath of Almighty God, and He asks, "Do you believe that I can safely carry you over to the other side? Do you really believe?"

There is a great amount of people around the world that respond with a loud, "Yes!" We say our prayers and visit church on Easter and Christmas. Many drop money into the offering plate; regularly attend Sunday school, and frequent services and mass. Many learn to prophesy in His name, cast out demons in His name, and they do wonderful works in the name of Jesus. Yet, through Jesus' Sermon on the Mount, we learn that those activities do not constitute true belief. Like the crowds, which came to watch Blondin, those activities are often nothing more than the rustlings of the masses that have gathered to be a part of the big show. And Jesus, just like the Great Blondin, is waving His nail-scarred hands over the masses, beckoning for our silence and saying, "If you really believe, get in the wheelbarrow."

When I tell the story of the Great Blondin, it often leaves people a bit perplexed. They look at me puzzled, and say, "Tony, I've heard about the cross; I've heard about the crown of thorns and the empty tomb; but I have not heard anything about a wheelbarrow." I quickly clarify that there is no magic or sacred wheelbarrow. I am simply using the story as a metaphor. It's a physical story, illustrating a spiritual point. The metaphor helps people to get spiritual, as well as mental, traction on what it means to believe.

Physically, what would someone need to do, in order to prove that he really believed the Great Blondin could cross Niagara Falls again? He would need to get out of the crowd, climb up the ladder, crawl into that wheelbarrow, sit really still, and put his faith and trust in the Great Blondin and his ability, to get him over to the other side safely. What is the spiritual equivalent to believing in Jesus? It is summed-up in a merging of Romans 10:9, "Confess with your mouth the Lord Jesus, and believe in you heart that God raised him from the dead, and you will be saved," with Luke 13:3, which says, "I tell you, unless you repent, you will all likewise perish." When you connect these two verses, you break the code to what it means to get into the wheelbarrow with Jesus.

Head-belief motivates you to serve, but heart-belief motivates you to surrender. The heart that surrenders is one that acts in repentance and faith. To repent is to hear the call of Christ and to respond to it in faith. Traversing the gamut of mental, emotional, and physical risks, that accompany the call of Christ, is the life of faith. Put those two ideas together, and you have the workings of what it means to trust. Any takers of Gravelet's invitation would have to trust him to carry them in that wheelbarrow. In the same way, if we are to be carried safely over into Heaven, it will require us to do our parts in repentance and faith, all the while trusting that God will do His part in extending mercy and grace. The Lord, Who—Alone—can take us safely over to the other side, is stretching out His hands, beckoning all of us to take our belief a step farther, put our faith and trust in Him, and surrender our lives to His Lordship.

The urgency of Jesus' message is staggering. It powerfully transcends, over the span of two thousand years, into our hearts today. It's staggering to think that people will stand before God on Judgment Day. Some will go to Heaven, but many will go to Hell. All of us will spend forever somewhere, and a heart belief is needed to make sure that your *somewhere* will be Heaven.

Chapter Twelve

Get In

Hit "Play," and let's take-in those last few minutes we enjoyed with Jesus on the Mount of Olives. The golden-brown canopy of dusk slowly dims, leaving in its absence silhouettes and shadows. Evening has come, bringing with it the charming, dancing flames of campfires and oil lamps. Crackling embers join the chorus of crickets, and the hearty aroma of roasting lamb tantalizes the senses. On any other night, the air would be filled with jovial chatter of family and friends, as they dine together and reminisce of the day's activities. Tonight, however, the atmosphere is saturated with a divine silence. People are thinking about and processing Jesus' *Early Edition* He delivered to them. The warm light of the campfire flickers across the faces of those staring into its core. These on-lookers' eyes are wide, jaws are taut, and their cheeks are streaked with tears. The teachings of Jesus moved the multitudes to think about where they stood, in their beliefs in God. His teachings seem to do that to people. Perhaps, His words have done the same to you.

Hit "Stop." This is where our journey back-in-time ends, and we find ourselves dealing honestly with reality. Just like His words did two thousand years ago, they also stir our hearts to consider our own spiritual conditions today. Right now, in this instant, I'm inviting you to evaluate where you are, in relationship to God's *Early Edition*. Do you know for certain that the story Jesus was telling is not about you? Nobody wants it to be about them, and the great point of the Gospel is that it doesn't have to be you! All you need to do is believe in your heart, get in the wheelbarrow, take God up on His invitation to "confess with your mouth the Lord Jesus, and believe in your heart."

At this present moment, I can lead you in a time of "confessing with your mouth." I can lead you in a time of prayer. You can read this prayer out loud, in a whisper, or in the silence of your mind, and God will hear you. He will extend His grace and mercy to you, carry you from this moment forward, and you can be prepared for Judgment Day. Before we pray, let me remind you that you are confessing with your mouth the "Lord" Jesus, not the icon Jesus, t-shirt Jesus, movie-star Jesus, jewelry-Jesus, or tattoo-Jesus. He is the "Lord Jesus!" You must be willing to surrender your life to Him as the leader, ruler, boss, and Lord of your life. Get out of the crowd of spectators, crawl into the wheelbarrow, giving Him full control over your entire life. When you are willing to do this, you have this promise in Romans 10:10 — "You will be saved." What awesome news!

To be clear, let me say that there is nothing magical about this prayer. Prayers don't save you; Jesus saves. However, praying to God is essential to making that connection, because prayer is the language of the soul to God. You can't call God on your cell phone.

You can't email or text-message Him, but He did text-message us, and in the sacred text of Scripture, He said in Romans 10:13, "Whoever calls upon the name of the Lord, shall be saved." Let me lead you in this moment, right now. Remember, you can read it out loud, in a whisper, or in the silence of your mind. Here's the prayer:

"Dear Jesus, I know that I am a sinner, and I am sorry for my sins. I thank You for Your 'Early Edition.' Your Word opened my eyes and heart. Right now, I believe that You are the sinless Son of God, and that You took my place on the cross for my sins. You poured out Your blood and died, You were buried; but three days later, You rose from the dead. That makes You Lord! Take my life; it's Yours. I'm in the wheelbarrow. From this moment on, help me to live for Your glory! In Jesus' Name, Amen!"

I am so stoked for all of you who just prayed that prayer! If you did, I want you to pay close attention to what I am about to tell you. I am about to give you some Biblical instruction, but the moment I do, spiritual warfare is going to bust out wherever you are. There is a real war going on for your soul. When I give you this instruction, you're going to find that your mind is going to be the target of two voices. One will be the voice of the devil, and he is going to create in your mind every reason in the world why you shouldn't do what I am about to instruct you to do. Don't listen to him! John 10:10 says that he wants to "steal, kill, and destroy" you. Let me say it again, don't listen to him! Instead, listen to Jesus, the other Voice, because He doesn't want to destroy you; rather, He wants to deliver you. In Psalm 50:15, He said, "I will deliver you." Listen to Jesus; He came to give you abundant life.

If you prayed that prayer, then you were saying that you got in the wheelbarrow, and Jesus is your Lord, which means you are going to do what He tells you to do. You are supposed to follow Him, and here is one of your first steps in following Jesus. In Matthew 10:32-33, Jesus said, "Whoever confesses Me before men, him I will also confess before My Father, Who is in heaven. But, whoever denies Me before men, him I will also deny before My

Father, Who is in heaven." Those are intense verses! I get people from all over the country who email, Tweet, or Facebook me, and want to know what those verses mean, and I have to be honest with them, as I will be honest with you. Although I have diagrammed and parsed the verbs, I do not know the full ramification of those verses. They are very mysterious to me. However, there is one thing clear about those verses, and it's this: if you prayed that prayer earlier, and if you really meant it, then you need to mention it. If you meant it, you will mention it! Jesus said, "Confess Him." He wants you to tell someone about your decision. This is not something that you tuck-away in your heart, treating it like some sort of "private thing" between you and God. It was a personal thing, but God never intended for it to be private. He wants you to tell the world. As a matter of fact, remember what He said in Matthew 10:32—"Confess me before men." Did you catch that? He said, "Before men." This means, He wants you to publicly declare what you said in private prayer.

Now, the devil is going to tell you not to do this. Don't listen to him; listen to Jesus. Jesus said to do it, so don't dismiss this as something small or of no consequence. It's a huge deal to God. Remember, He said, "If you deny Me, I will deny you." That's straight up serious, so here is what you need to do. Right now, go find someone and tell him you have given your life to Jesus. That's right, I said to do it right now. Perhaps, you're on a subway. If so, just tap the person next to you, and tell him. Maybe you are at a coffee shop. Look around you. Is there anybody else in there with you? How about that person, who made your coffee? Go tell her you gave your life to Christ Jesus. Perhaps, you are home with family. Go find them, and share this news! Don't be ashamed. Confess Him, by telling somebody!

Everything I have shared with you in this book, I have preached in churches and arenas across America. Right now, at this point in the message in an arena-, camp-, or church-setting, I invite every-body who prayed to stand up and shout that Jesus is their Lord. How's that for a "confess Him" moment? Then, I invite them to step out of the crowd, walk up to the platform where I am standing, and let everybody in that place know that they meant every word of what they said. Do they come? Oh, yeah! They roll out of their seats in great numbers! I've seen hundreds of thousands publicly declare what they said in private prayer. To God be the glory!

Remember Blondin? What did someone need to do, to prove it to him? That's right, he had to get out of the crowd and take a radical, public step, wide-open in the public. You can go and tell someone. Come on, you can do this, and after you do, then I would encourage you to do two things. First, if someone gave you this book as a gift, then text, email, or call them, letting them know that you have believed Christ in your heart. Second, I want you to find a place of worship, and go make your decision public there. Why should you do that? Well, it's what Christ wants you to do. Most of the New Testament was written to instruct people on how to live as a Church family. Hebrews 10:25 says, "Not forsaking the assembling of ourselves together, as is the manner of some, but exhorting one another, and so much the more, as you see the Day approaching." Plus, it will prove to secure you some incredible blessings. You will also gain a

connection-point with fellow-believers, who will be in your balcony,

cheering you on through community. That's just the start of this new

journey. A whole new purpose and direction in life awaits you.

Chapter Thirteen

Now, What?

As you read the story about the tightrope-walker and Niagara Falls, did it stir a question within you, like it did me? When I first heard the story, I immediately wondered if anyone took Blondin up on his offer. Did the whole crowd stand there with an eye-averting, "don't-look-at- me" expression on their faces? Or could there have been, among the thousands of spectators, someone who dared to get in that wheelbarrow? Sitting on a wooden pew, in a Baptist church, I got my answer to this question. I was listening to a preacher, and in the middle of his message, he began telling the story about the Great Blondin. I thought to myself, "I know this story, and it's a great illustration for heart belief." The minister did not take that angle, but instead he fast forwarded the story to the ending. Just after the preacher quoted Blondin's famous question, he paused for a few breaths, looked all of us in the eyes, and said something I never knew about the story. He said that a reporter for a local newspaper took Gravelet up on his invitation. Hundreds of other reporters stood in the crowd and watched, as one of their own sat white-knuckled, gripping the sides of the wheelbarrow, which was suspended on a rope over the raging waters. As the story goes, he made it safely over to the other side.

In 1859, newspapers were the internet of that day. Little boys, wearing worn out wool caps, would stand on street corners, peddling the papers. The day following Blondin's Niagara crossing, the tiny scrappy paperboys couldn't keep up with the demand. Everybody wanted to read about the fantastic story. After giving a dime, curious patrons flipped through all of the pages. There were many stories within the paper about the stunt, but they got overlooked or discarded. There was only one account that people wanted to read. They weren't interested in hearing from the reporters, who watched it. They wanted to hear from the guy, who got into the wheelbarrow. That seemed to be the only story that mattered to them, and it's easy to understand why.

I have found this same dynamic happens in the world of spiritual matters. I got in the wheelbarrow with Jesus, back in 1989. I hope you have a time, when you got in. Perhaps, it was the day you read chapter twelve of this book. There are lots of exciting and enriching things that happen, when you trust Christ. One of them, is that people will notice and will want to read your story. The world is sick of hearing from people, who are merely observing Christianity from the sidelines. They want to hear from the ones, who have dared to take God up on His offer. That's what you and I have done, and now we have something to tell our neighbors, co-workers, and classmates. It's the story of God and His great salvation. The rest of this book will be a journey on how to tell this God-story well, so that others experience His love, and you bring glory to Jesus.

First things first, let's deal with the topic of confidence. It's important to understand that we are not sharing the story of how great we are at sitting in the wheelbarrow. It's not about us. We are sharing the story of the amazing ability of God to forgive our sins and save our souls. The story is about the Tightrope-Walker, Jesus. The big news is about how able He is to carry us, and we can tell the story, like no one else, because we are in that journey with Jesus over to the other side. It's all about Him and His amazing ability; so, right off-the-bat, we need to have a confident, solid understanding in God's ability to get us over to the other side.

If we take the metaphor with the tightrope-walker a bit farther, then what does it look like for us to sit still in the wheelbarrow with God pushing us, as the reporter did with Gravelet? Psalm 46:10 states that we are to "be still and know that He is God." This does not mean that we are to be passive, lazy, and disengaged. It is simply saying that we are to rest in and trust that the God, Who said He would save us, will in fact, save us! It's our responsibility to live each day in praise to God, worshipping the One, Who is saving us. We are to love God and to love people—not in an effort to earn our salvation, but in response to God for His extending salvation to us.

When we do this, people will want to read our stories, and we will be able to tell them about the amazing, life-saving ability of Jesus Christ.

The Christian experience is trusting God to do what He said He would do. You called on Him, and He said He will save. God will always do what He says He will do. If you confessed Him before men, then He will confess you on Judgment Day. He will do what He said He will do. You can sit still, as you travel the tightrope of life safely in the hands of a capable, great God. You can rest assured He has more skills than Blondin ever thought about having; and you will make it. In the Gospel of John 10:28-29, Jesus said, "And I give them eternal life, and they shall never perish; neither shall anyone snatch them out of My hand. My Father, Who has given them to Me, is greater than all; and no one is able to snatch them out of My Father's hand." This means, you are in good and capable hands. You did your part of repentance and faith, and now you must confidently trust God to do His part.

This is a crucial element of the story we are telling others, because, like we learned from the people Jesus was talking about in His Sermon on the Mount, there are no works that will get you into Heaven. You can only come through the work of God, and it's one He can deliver-on, as the apostle Paul said in Philippians 1:6, "Being confident of this very thing, that He who has begun a good work in you will complete it until the day of Jesus Christ." Did you see that word Paul used? It was the word *confident*. God will do what He says! You and I can confidently trust Him, and you will need this confidence in order to deal with the next topic that needs to be engaged.

The topic I am referring to is called, "Follow-up." Follow-up is a practice that church leaders and ministers want to make sure happens in the life of someone, who has just believed the claims of Christ in his heart. It was a mandate from Jesus, given to us in Matthew 28:19-20. He said, "Go therefore and make disciples of all the nations, baptizing them in the name of the Father, and of the Son, and of the Holy Spirit, teaching them to observe all things that

I have commanded you." Follow-up is a moment, when we want to ensure that you leverage all God has promised to you in His Word, so that you maximize your new life in Christ, and become a fully-devoted follower of Jesus.

Earlier, I mentioned that the devil is out to steal, kill, and destroy you. You need to be aware that the moment you get saved, he unleashes an all-out assault against you. He wants to steal the faith you have in your heart. The Word of God is our source of faith, and satan wants to snatch it out of our hearts. Jesus spoke about the devil's tactics in a parable about a farmer sowing seeds, and how the birds of the air came and stole them out of the soil. In Luke 8:11-12, Jesus said, "The seed is the word of God....the devil comes and takes away the word out of their hearts, lest they should believe." Being aware that this attack happens, it's important that you are ministered to, or followed-up with. Spiritual leaders want to "shoo" the devil off, like a crow from in a garden, and nurture the seed that's in the soil of your heart. That process is called, "Follow-up." You can see why this is so important to your spiritual growth.

Throughout the rest of the book, you will take a journey that will give you more than enough practical steps to arm yourself against the devil's attacks and to nurture your spiritual growth. To start this expedition, I want to share one of the most important words I can give you, as you begin your journey of trusting Jesus. If you miss this instruction, it will cause you great distress and spiritual set-backs. Pay close attention to what I am about to say. Are you listening? Okay, here it is. As much as the Bible emphasizes *follow-up*, it also has an emphasis on *follow-through*. This one core principle is a serious game-changer for living the Christian life. That being the case, let's take some time and unwrap what it means.

Chapter Fourteen

Follow-Through

I t would serve us well for me to repeat myself at the start of this important chapter. As much as there is an emphasis on *follow-up* in the Bible, there is also an emphasis on *follow-through*. I told you what *follow-up* was; now, let's look at *follow-through*.

In Mark 8:34, Jesus said, "Whoever desires to come after Me, let him deny himself, and take up his cross, and follow Me." He also said, in Luke 9:62, "No one, having put his hand to the plow, and looking back, is fit for the kingdom of God." Do you feel the sense of personal involvement being stressed in these words of Christ? You see, *follow-up* is about the Church helping you, and *follow -through* is about your helping yourself. Yes, the Church will be there for you, but it won't, and can't, live-out this life for you. You prayed, and, with your lips, you made a confession that Jesus is your Lord. Now, you must *follow-through* with your life. This is essential to embrace, if you are to experience the abundant life Christ has for you, in the days ahead.

The Apostle Paul has a strong word about this for us. Essentially, he is saying to all of us, who have believed (and really meant it), that we should follow-through with our commitment. In Colossians 3:8, he tells us to "put off... anger, wrath, malice, blasphemy, and filthy language." And in verse 12, he says we are to "put on tender mercies, kindness, humility, meekness, and long-suffering." Do you see the follow-through element? Because our lives are "hidden in Christ" (It's all about Him.), then we should put-off certain activities and put-on certain virtues.

You have an active role in Christ's work that God is doing in you; the work He said He would complete. This is different from the works the people did in Christ's story, who did not make it into Heaven. They were very busy outside the wheelbarrow, standing among the crowd, acting as if they were in the wheelbarrow, and God declared that their works were lawless deeds. Paul is saying that once you are in Christ (you've "gotten in the wheelbarrow," trusting His finished-work on the cross), now you are to follow-through practically with where you are positionally. Positionally, you are in His hands, and practically, you are to live like it: putting-off sin and putting-on attributes through the power of the Holy Spirit that will tell the story of Jesus.

Over the years, I have spoken and counseled with multitudes of people about following- through. I have a plethora of resources to pull from that I use to help them, but the longer I live, the more intense my desire becomes to have things streamlined and simpli-fied. It's with this mindset, that I dove into all those resources and found one set of verses that I think could help you to do your part, and trust God to do His. These are verses I had in mind, when I spoke earlier about the journey we would be taking together, that would arm you against the devil's attacks and nurture your spiritual growth.

Before we get into those verses, however, I need to make sure you are awake for the journey. The rest of this book calls for your full-attention. In the next few chapters, we will be going on an exhilarating spiritual excursion through some of the most popular verses in the Bible, but you must make sure you are awake and energized for the trip. I say this, because one of the most frustrating things I experience when helping others, is their tendencies to let their attention doze-off, and to put their passions on-snooze. Instead of enjoying life, they are enduring it. It stresses me out, to think about all of the tragic stories I've heard over the years. Marriages that end in divorce; stepchildren that go-off the deep-end; students, who take a shortcut, and their lives are cut-short; and the list goes on and on. When it comes to following-through, it's not a cliché; it's really true: when you snooze, you lose!

I heard a story about a little boy, whose parents tucked him into bed. Dressed in his soft pajamas, he sank into his fluffy covers and snuggled with his teddy bear. As the child lay close to the teddy, with his arm dangling over the side of the bed, stroking his pet-cat's back, his mother prayed (what the boy considered) the longest bed-time prayer in the world. Once she finished, the cat raced away; she kissed her son's forehead and turned-off the light, as she exited the room. Once she got back downstairs, she picked-up where she had left off in her gardening magazine.

Not less than ten minutes later, she heard a frightening thud on the floor upstairs. She leaped out of her chair, and she dashed up the stairs to her son's room. In haste, she flung open the door, and a slice of the hallway light pierced the darkness, revealing an empty bed! Anxiously, she fumbled for the light-switch. Her fingers navigated the wall, feeling the cold brass switch plate, then the holes and the crease of the screws holding it in place. Finally, she reached the switch, which did not move, as she nervously pressed it downward. She reversed the motion, and the singular incandescent bulb in the middle of the ceiling flickered on. The increased light confirmed her fears. Her boy was gone!

In his place was the teddy and his covers, stretching over the side of the bed and onto the floor. Her heart pounded within her chest, and a cold flush swept over her body, from head to toe. She started to scream for her husband, when, suddenly, the pile of covers on the floor began to move. Rolling from beneath the cascading covers, came her little child. His eyes, seeking relief from the light, were squinting tightly, as he rubbed the back of his head, nursing a rather large goose-egg. Startled, the mother exclaimed, "Son, what happened to you!" The boy sheepishly replied with a groan, "I don't know, Mom. I guess I fell asleep too close to where I got in."

I am no expert, but my observations tell me that this is a very real danger for all those, who are trusting Jesus. Jesus is the One carrying us, He is doing the work for our salvation; and if unguarded, this inherently leads to a slumbering form of follow-through. In my twenty years of ministry, I've watched people snuggle under the covers of Christ's atonement and fall asleep right where they got in. Just like the boy in the bedtime story, this kind of activity leads to a painful fall. I've spent countless hours helping people nurse the wounds they received from their tumbles, and when I open God's word to help them find the remedy for their pain, they can't handle the Light. They emotionally and mentally squint, and it takes a long time for their spiritual eyes to adjust. It's no wonder that the Apostle Paul sounded the alarm, and, in 1 Corinthians 15:34, he said, "Awake to righteousness." You've gotten in the wheelbarrow; you're saved. —Just don't fall asleep there. 2 Peter 1:5 says, "Giving all diligence, add to your faith." Peter is not saying that the Gospel isn't enough and that there are some other things you need to do, to save your soul. In verses one through four, he declares the power of the Gospel to fully save our souls. Now, in verse five, he is saying, since it is the case that God will deliver us from this world of corruption, don't fall asleep! Rather, put forth maximum effort; engage your faith in deeds that prove you are not a passive spectator to God's amazing salvation, but that you are a partaker of it. Like the half-brother of Jesus said, in James 2:18, "I will show you my faith by my works."

For all of us, who dare to climb-in, stay alert and be engaged; life will be an adventure of unprecedented-highs and spiritual victories. Following-through is a spectacular feat, one that will draw the attention of your co-workers, classmates, friends, and family members. They will want to read your story, and it's one that will point them to a loving, gracious, and saving God—the Lord Jesus Christ. It's time to follow-through. Let's go for it.

Chapter Fifteen

Twenty-Eight Words

I've been asked, if I could only share two verses from the Bible that would merge the whole follow-up and follow-through dynamic, what would they be? That may sound like a tall order, but I think I have two. However, I don't recommend your limiting your whole Christian experience to just two verses from the Bible. You have the whole Bible, so I would encourage you to read the whole thing. I make it a practice to read through the Bible every year. It's filled with principles and steps to help us pull life off and to live for the glory of God, so I'm a fan for using your whole Bible!

At a conference I attended several years ago, one of the speakers gave an awesome illustration about having the Word of God and using it. When he was in high school, he loved fall, because it brought with it the awesome game of football. His school team was actually pretty bad, but they had a weapon that made them winners. It did not matter how awful they were at the other areas of their game, every time they got into a third down situation, they never feared, because they knew they could get a first down. They had a three-hundred-and-twenty-pound boy, whom they would hand the ball off to, and with players piled on his back and legs, he would walk to the first down mark! Every tough third down situation, the cheerleaders would call for them to unleash their secret weapon. Cheering with pom-poms waving in the air, they would chant, "You've got it, now use it! You've got it, now use it! You've got it, now use it!"

The Bible is no secret, but it is a weapon! Ephesians 6:17 calls it "the sword of the Spirit." It is mighty in Truth, that moves you forward-upfield in this journey, called life. Don't neglect your Bible! We've got it, and we are going to use it! I've encouraged you to read the whole thing systematically every year, but for the purposes of this book, I want to share two powerful verses that will change your life. These verses will mightily merge *follow-up* and *follow-through*. They capture the whole idea of your doing your part and God's doing His. They are found in the third chapter of the book of Proverbs, verses five and six.

"Trust in the Lord with all of your heart, And lean not unto your own understanding. In all your ways acknowledge Him and He shall direct your paths."

I mentioned earlier that these two verses are some of the most popular verses in the Bible. They seem to be everywhere we look. I've seen them on bumper stickers, t-shirts, Bible covers, paintings; and I've even seen them on dinner plates. It's kind of cool that they get so much eye-time with us, but I think the point of the writer of Proverbs is that they would get heart-time. It's great that they are popular, but our lives are only changed by them, when they are practiced.

These twenty-eight words streamline the millions of instructions we find throughout the entire Bible. Again, I invite you to follow my lead and read your Bible through every year, but what I am saying, is that these verses pack a powerful amount of insights about living and evoking God's redemptive intervention in our daily affairs. The thing I love the most about them, is that they help you handle any and every problem you will ever face. That may sound like an exaggerated claim, but I assure you, it's not. I am so stoked, because, as you continue to read this book, you are going to find out just how true that statement is.

Problems are like terrorists that try to hijack our faith. They ambush new believers and get them to second-guess the promises of God and their commitment to Him. We all face problems, but we all handle them differently. Here's a question that I'd like for you answer. How do you handle problems in your life? Before you give me your answer, let me expand the question. How do you handle problems in your life, so that you get the victory over your problems, and your problems don't get the victory over you? We all know that there are right ways and wrong ways to handling our problems. I recall when I was a seven-year-old boy, such a moment that didn't go so well.

I am, by nature, very hyper. ADD doesn't even begin to describe me. I don't just bite my fingernails, I bite other people's fingernails. (I'm doing better with it these days, but when I was young, I was out of control.) On one occasion, my energy got the best of me. I ran into a major problem: I got flat-out bored! So, to solve my problem of boredom, I went into the kitchen and grabbed a pack of matches. Then, I proceeded to go into my neighbor's backyard and start, what began as, a small fire. It seemed to work! I piled up a mound of dry leaves, lit the match, tossed it in, and my boredom seemed to float away, as the red, yellow, and orange flames licked toward the heavens. I threw a few other things that were lying around the backyard, onto the pile, and they went up in flames, as well. It was thrilling! It really got exciting when the fire-trucks showed up!

I was instantly locked in my room and told that I had to stay there, until my dad came home. Anticipation about a spanking has a way of making the discipline all the more memorable. Well, when Dad got off work that night, we had a very convincing meeting about why that was not a good way to solve my problem of boredom. Let's just say my rear got so hot from his belt, I thought we were going to have to call the fire-trucks back, to cool down my backside! Like I said, there are right ways and wrong ways to handling your problems. How do you handle your problems, so that you get the win over your problems, and your problems don't end up defeating you?

We all have problems, and yours may not be that you start fires out of boredom. If it is, then you need to know I am feeling you here; however, let me encourage you not to do it! Firemen frown on it, and your dad may come close to killing you. One thing I do know, from reading 1 Peter 5:8, is that the devil is prowling around, like a blood-thirsty lion, "seeking whom he may devour." Satan will take every opportunity to leverage life's difficulties against you. He delights in getting us to take a wrong step in handling our problems; and, before we know it, we've started a relational fire, an occupational fire, or an infidelity fire. Now, instead of enjoying peace and victory, we are walking around nursing the wounds from the third-degree burns on our hearts.

I am focusing on problem-solving for our follow-up study, because it is the game-changer, when it comes to your and my following-through with our believing in Jesus. Problems can stop you dead in your tracks, and solving them effectively can keep you on the right track. Proverbs 3:5-6 breaks the code to effectively handling every problem we will ever face. In these verses, Solomon lays out three steps for us to take, in our decision-making processes. When we do these three things, the results are supernatural! Go grab a coffee, make sure you're wide awake, because I'm about to do a little follow-up with you. We are going to take a journey through these verses, and if you put them into practice, you will be on your way to following-through in a lifestyle of living-out your belief in our great God, Who is mighty to save!

Chapter Sixteen

Attach

The twenty-eight words that compose this popular Proverb came from the mouth of Solomon, but were birthed from the mind of God. 2 Peter 1:21 says that Scripture came as men were "moved by the Holy Spirit." Therefore, this powerful problem-solving procedure was given to us by God, Himself. Knowing this, fuels our confidence that it will work.

The very first step we are told to take is to trust. He says, "Trust in the Lord." The word "trust" is the Hebrew word, *batach*, which means to attach oneself to something with confident assurance. He is admonishing us to cling, to stick, or to adhere to God. I think we all know that if we have an issue in life that we should run to

God, but have you really thought about God? Are we really thinking about Whom Solomon is telling us to attach ourselves to? We are talking about the God of the universe.

No one has taught me more about the greatness of God than Louie Giglio. His book, <u>i am not, but i know I AM,</u> is my all-time favorite. Outside of the Bible, no other book has changed my life more significantly. I strongly encourage you to look that book up and purchase it for your library. He also has a DVD of an anointed message that he preached, called "How Great is Our God." I encourage you to get that, as well. Both of these resources will blow your ever-loving mind to the awe-inspiring, majestic awesomeness of God. I'll let Louie be our guide on those matters; but if you'll permit me, I would like to give a little insight on one attribute of God that I find helpful in this problem-solving procedure.

One of the things that I love about God is that He is a Covenant-Keeper. He doesn't break His word; He always keeps His promises. The world, for the most part, knows very little about keeping covenants. We change our hearts about things, as quickly as we can change our minds. It's sad, really. I've been emotionally crushed by the fickle promises of others, and I bet you have, too. We've all had people make big promises, only to deliver bigger pains. In contrast, God isn't like that; He is a Covenant-Keeper. Being a covenant-keeper is a massively big deal.

To really get what this whole, big-covenant-keeper-thing is all about, we need to rewind our time-machine a little farther back, than the date for the Sermon on the Mount. We have to go back farther than two thousand years. Let's go back to a period between 625 BC and 536 BC. It was a dark time during the Babylonian (Chaldean) Empire. Jeremiah was called by God to preach to the people of Judah. There is a verse in the book of Jeremiah that gives a little insight to what went on, when making or keeping a covenant. Jeremiah 34:18 states, "…The words of the covenant which they made before Me, when they cut the calf in two, and passed between the parts of it."

At first glance, we miss what's going on here, but let's look a little deeper, and I think, what we will see, will astound you. A basic definition of a covenant is a solemn agreement. In the Old Testament, when two people were going to make an agreement together, they had an interesting ceremony that carried a powerful and seriously symbolic meaning with it. Let's just say you and I were neighbors back in 550 BC, and we wanted to agree to protecting each other's land from bandits. What would that look like?

Normally, there would be a simple, written invitation that would discuss the agreement. A date would be set to publicly meet and seal the covenant, and we would both be required to bring a few witnesses with us. We would meet in an open field on the set-date, and, along with the witnesses, someone would bring a lamb. The lamb would be killed, and then it would be cut in-half. The two pieces of the carcass would be laid on the ground, about two feet apart from one another. We would walk in-between those pieces and begin our ceremony to seal-the-deal. We would stand in the midst of the wiggling bundle of lamb flesh, bend our knees, and put ourselves into a half-squatted position, facing one another. As we are in the squat-position, we would take our right hands and grab one

another's inner right thighs. (Seems a bit awkward, and I don't recommend trying this the next time you greet visitors in your church.)
While in this position, we would look each other in the eyes, and we
would state our agreement out-loud. It would be something simple
like, "As your neighbor, I promise to protect your land, as you look
after mine." Then, we would release our grips, stand up, and walk
away. This may sound a little sketchy, but it packed a lot of punch.

You see, in making this covenant, we were essentially saying
that if either of us did not live up to our agreement, then the other
party would have permission to do to us what was done to the lamb.
That's intense; that's serious, and that's called a covenant! Now,
think about the fact that God is a Covenant-Keeper with us. He did
butcher a Lamb, to make an agreement with us, and He will never
go-back on His word! Now, when we hear this admonition to attach
ourselves to God, it should create hope and peace in our hearts,
knowing that Jehovah is a covenant- keeping God, Who will never
go-back on His word.

The extent of this exhortation is to do it *with all of our hearts*. The Hebrew word, used for "heart," is *leb*. It's defined as the soul, or the seat, of your appetites. It's referring to the thing in you that makes you tick. He is telling us to attach ourselves to God with everything within us. The thing I have discovered from ministering to so many different people, is that most of us know to do this, when we face problems. Chances are, you already knew this. I am not telling you anything new here. I agree this is not rocket-science, and we are not splitting atoms here; but it does require a little thinking, or else you will miss the underlying, significant principle in this first step. Here it is: if we are to attach ourselves to God with all of our hearts, then it presumes that we must also detach ourselves from everything else that's not of God. You can't grab-hold of God, when your fists are full of other stuff. You have to let go of some things. Failure to get this right, could result in our suffering the African monkey's fate. Let me explain.

I had a friend, who went on a mission trip to Africa, where he met some of the nicest people he had ever encountered. They were giving and kind, had a devout sense of true community; and my friend grew to love them. They did, however, have one thing that was a bit unsettling about them. They ate monkeys. I'm not sure how you just responded to that last sentence, but I can tell you that if it did not cause you to grimace, then please don't ever invite me over to your house for dinner. I don't do cats, and I don't eat monkeys. (Yuck! —That would be a big cultural-shock for me. I could never handle pulling up to McDonald's to order a milkshake, French fries, and a McMonkey sandwich. I'm not doing it!) It's kind of crazy that they eat monkeys, but it's fascinating how they catch them.

The hunt begins by developing a trap, made with a small, clay jar. It's designed with a wide bottom and a small opening at the top, just big enough for a monkey to squeeze his hand through it. Next, the hunters bait the traps with peanuts. After filling a dozen jars, they bury them with the bottom down and top up, so that the patch of earth looks like an area with a bunch of small holes in the ground. Then, the hunter grabs a large stick, and he hides in the nearby bush.

It doesn't take long, and the monkey detects the scent of the nuts. It races over, reaches into the jar, and grabs a fist-full of lunch. The hunter quickly jumps out of the shrubs, takes a big swing, and it's lights-out for the monkey. —Sort of ingenious of the hunter and really stupid of the monkey. The monkey's fist could easily fit through the opening in the jar, but not while gripping his food-score. You see, the monkey could have escaped his terrible fate, but he failed to do so, because he would not let his treasure go.

The devil is much like those hunters. He is relentless in his attempts to ensnare us. I've learned that when we face problems in life, God invites us to trust Him. But in the same instance, satan will also offer us something that appears to be very promising. I would caution you to consider the monkey story and beware of the devil's traps. Solomon says to cling to God with *all of our hearts*. Let go of everything else, and put a two-fisted grip on the Covenant-Keeping God of the Universe. Once we have done this, it's on to step two.

Chapter Seventeen

Avoid

The next step in this procedure is to *lean not on your own understanding*. The word "lean" depicts an attitude of trust. It denotes the action of relying upon something or someone. He is telling us to not rely on or trust in our own understanding. Since this is a crucial step in the problem-solving process, it would do us good to have an understanding about what he means, when he uses the word "understanding." What is he talking about?

The transliteration of the Hebrew word is *biynah*. This word refers to our intelligence or our abilities to have mental insight. One might even suggest that it speaks of logic. It's the same word we find in the question asked in Job 38:36—"Who has given understanding to the heart?" When you break this down, it refers to your and my knowing what is best for our lives, minus God. It's talking about our abilities to know what is best for our lives, without any prayer, Bible- study, or godly counsel. To put it in a modern-day vernacular, Solomon is saying, "Don't go there!"

The first time I heard this, I immediately questioned it. I was thinking that we humans are pretty smart. We have invented every-thing from the wheel to the artificial heart. Why does God not want us using our heads? He is the One, Who stated through the prophet in Isaiah 1:18— "Come now and let us reason together." God gave us the capacity to think, and now we are not *supposed* to use it? I think God wants us to use it, but He doesn't want us to do so, without His influence and insights. When we operate from our own understandings, we are essentially saying that we know what is best for our lives, more than God does. When we operate our lives like that, it could be fatal.

Proverbs 14:12 and 16:25 say the same thing. They read, "There is a way that seems right to a man, but its end is the way of death."

God says this twice, because its truth is so vital, and He doesn't want us to miss it. When we live in light of what we think is best for our lives, it could cost us our lives. I know people, who have made decisions outside of prayer, God's Word, or godly counsel, and it literally cost them their lives. I'm thinking right now of a girl, who hung-out with some friends that God's Word said she should not let influence her. (1 Corinthians 15:33 says, "Evil company corrupts good habits.") Her godly parents also told her to avoid them, but she did not listen. One night, when her friends were intoxicated, she got in the car with them, they wrecked, and she died. How tragic! Don't operate on what *you* think is best, because it could be fatal.

Most of the time when we make choices without God's influence, it doesn't always cost us our lives. Truth is, most of us do that, and we go on living, breathing, and moving into the future. It doesn't always prove to be fatal, but I have learned that it always proves to be foolish—it's not without consequences. You see, when we operate from what we think is best for our lives, we always miss God's best for our lives. When we limit ourselves to our own understanding of the way things are, or should be, we miss-out on what God has for us.

One of my favorite characters in history is Christopher Columbus. There were a lot of things he did in his life that I don't agree with; however, I do admire him for his faith, leadership, and boldness as a sailor. First of all, he was radical, almost to the point that others thought he was crazy. (I've learned that it helps to be a little crazy.) One radical thing he had going for him was that he believed the Bible through and through, even if it meant going against-the-grain of what everyone else thought.

An example of his radical mindset can be seen in his understanding of the shape of the earth. In his day, the common belief about the shape of the world was that it was flat. However, Christopher thought it was round. He was not the only one to believe this, nor was he the one to discover it to be true. Many people before him, including Aristotle, held to a spherical earth; but the vast majority of people, during this time, believed it to be flat. Armed with Isaiah 40:22, which tells us that God "sits above the circle of the earth,"

Christopher was determined to sail to new lands that awaited discovery on the other side of the earth's curvature.

Most people laughed and mocked him for his ideas. Other captains jeered him, thought his vision was absurd, and they never believed that his voyage would get the needed-investors to sponsor its deployment. However, Queen Isabella, of Spain, gave him—not one, not two—but three ships. Money would not be the difficulty for his quest; his problem was in getting a crew.

As I mentioned earlier, some educated individuals were inclined to think that the world was round, but most common people did not think so. Deck-hand sailors were about as common- folk as you could get in the 1400s. They were certain the earth was flat, and if you sailed to its edge, you would fall-off into a dark firmament or abyss. Nevertheless, Columbus went door-to-door, campaigning and recruiting for his dream-voyage.

The day came for Columbus to loose the moorings and set-sail on his journey. Did you know that on that day, there were many people who were asked to go, but didn't? Instead, they stayed on the dock and on dry land. Do you know what they did? Those people limited themselves to their understanding of the shape of the earth. On the other hand, there were others, who did not limit themselves, but dared to get off the dock and into the ship. These brave souls set-sail on the greatest adventure of their lives. Although they encountered hardships and made some horrible choices in other areas of their lives, when one looks at the big picture, they made history for the glory of God! When I think of that kind of history, and in light of Proverbs 3:5, it causes me to exclaim that we should all jump off the dock of doubt, hop into the ship of Christianity, hoist the sails of faith; fill them with the wind of the Word of God; set-sail on the greatest adventure of our lives; and make history for the glory of our great covenant-keeping God!

This is not a new idea for you. You have already proven that you aren't one to just go with the majority and miss out on an invitation from God. You got out of the crowd, and you jumped into the wheelbarrow with Jesus. You have already broken the barrier of being limited by your own understanding. But as you continue in this journey of trusting and following Jesus, there will be times, when what He asks you to do, won't make sense. From one fellow wheelbarrow-rider to another, let me encourage you to keep trusting Him. He is a Covenant-Keeper, and He won't back-down from His part of the deal. He will use you to tell His story, and that's the core of history, isn't it? It's His-Story. I know you are all in, so grab the riggings and hoist the sails of faith! Let's fill them with the Word of God and check-out the last step in this problem-solving procedure.

Chapter Eighteen

Acknowledge

S olomon closes-out this admonition with the greatest of chal-
lenges: "In all your ways acknowledge Him." I have found
this to be the most arduous of the three steps. Most of the Christians
that I do life with, agree that it's very demanding. It may be difficult, but as we will see in the closing chapters of this book, it's also
extraordinarily rewarding. Let's break this step down, so we can
know how to step it up.

The word for "ways," in Hebrew, is *derek;* it speaks of our man-
ners or habits. Its etymology leads us to believe that it's referring to
the course of action of our lives, which is to say, our lifestyles. The

habit or manner that he is asking us to embrace is one of acknowledging the Lord. This is the tough part I was talking about.

When we think of acknowledging someone, we tend to think about saying hello or waving at them. We do this when passing by a friend, whom we happen to notice, while driving-up the road in our cars. When we see him, we honk and wave. That is one form of acknowledging someone. However, the word acknowledge in this text is much more intense than that. He is not telling us to buddy-up with God and simply give Him a cordial nod. The Hebrew word is "yada`," which is an imperative command. (Remembering that Scripture is given by God, we are to understand that it's God, through the writing of Solomon, Who is giving us this command. This is not a suggestion.) "Yada`" embodies the act of admitting or submitting. Its placement here in Proverbs carries the idea that we are to submissively obey the Lord. Did you catch that? It's not enough that we simply obey God. We are to *submissively* obey Him.

I heard a story about a mother, who had her little four-and-a-half-year-old boy with her, while grocery shopping. Her child went bonkers, as she strolled down the breakfast cereal aisle. His eyes

spotted a colorful box of sugar-loaded, yummy stuff that he really

wanted. He jumped to his feet in the cart seat, with his finger pointed

toward the box, and screamed at the top of his lungs, "I want that

one!" She sat him down and gave him a sweet, "No, honey, it's not

healthy to have that much sugar. Mommy is getting this one." She

was holding a plain brown box of fiber flakes. His eyes dialed-in on

another mother, who grabbed the box he wanted and put it into her

cart. He stood up and protested, "But, Mom, that other mommy is

getting the yummy one for her child!" She gently sat him back down

and kept rolling, up the aisle. The little girl, who was riding in the

cart that scored the box of cereal he wanted, stuck her thumbs in

her ears, and while wiggling her fingers, she stuck-out her tongue,

taunting him.

He stood back up and yelled again, "I want the other one!"

The mother tucked him back into the cart seat; but he immediately

jumped back up, pointed at the taunting girl, and screamed even

louder. Again, the mother sat him back down, only to have him scream and stand back up. This time, the mother did a little-five-finger, palm-of-the-hand "counseling session" with him. After a few rapid-fire whacks on his bottom, she firmly put him back in his seat, and got back to her shopping. After a few minutes, she glanced at her boy and was taken aback by his disposition. He was sitting in the seat with his arms crossed and his face in a furious frown. In full-pout, his bottom lip pursed over his top lip, and his eyes squinted, seething with anger. She asked, "What in the world is the matter with you, Boy?" He abruptly barked, "Momma, I might be sitting down on the outside, but I'm standing up on the inside!"

My personal experience has taught me that I have the tendency to do this with God. He asks me to obey Him with some matter, and it doesn't sit quite right with me emotionally or mentally, and I find myself acting like that little boy. I obey, but my attitude is negative, and I'm standing up on the inside. Perhaps you can identify with me. Solomon is saying, we need to be people, who acknowledge God by sitting down on the inside, as well as on the outside. God is not wanting us to acquiesce; He wants us to acknowledge.

Are we to do this in just a few of our ways? Are we told to do this only on special religious holidays? Is the command only required of us on Sundays? This may be the way a lot of "so-called" Christians live for God, but it's not how we have been commanded. We are to acknowledge Him in *all of our ways*. This means every day and in every area of our lives. This is intense stuff!

There are moments we read about in history that have a way of marking and inspiring us. I read something about a Spanish explorer that gave me a deeper insight about this concept of *all your ways*. The explorer was Hernándo Cortés, and his fierce fighting skills and radical, sailing-heart led him to fame. He is most infamous for conquering the Aztecs, who were brutal people, reportedly offering 84,000-human sacrifices in four days, at the consecration of the Great Pyramid of Tenochtitlan, in 1847. However horrifying this may be to us, it did not merit the massacres that followed by Cortés. Please hear me out—I am in no way condoning what this Conquistador did, in killing these people. I just find his skills, as a leader, very interesting and noteworthy.

On April 12, 1519, Cortés and a band of followers on a fleet of eleven Spanish galleons, dropped-anchor off the coast of Vera Cruz. Before entering small dinghies to row ashore, Captain Hernándo gave the order for all the crew and soldiers to burn the ships. Yes, that's right, he told them to burn the ships. Talk about a great time-machine moment to visit; that would be awesome! I would love to have seen the looks on their faces, after hearing this command. Maybe nobody said it out-loud, because they valued their lives, but somebody had to be thinking, "Did the waves get you discombobulated? Was the rum a bit strong? 'Burn the Ships?' —Really?! You have lost your ever-loving mind!" And one might have concluded that the Captain *had* lost his mind, until he or she discovered what that act accomplished. They did burn the ships, every last one of them, including the Captain's; and when they did, it eliminated any opportunity for them to turn back from the quest they had resolved to conquer. That, right there, is what you call a radical commitment!

If you ask me, I think their obsession with power and riches were sinful and, ultimately, got the best of them. However, what could happen, if that kind of resolve were poured into living for the glory of God? I think that is exactly the kind of radical invitation we are getting from Solomon, here in Proverbs—*in all of your ways, acknowledge God.*

As I've mentioned earlier, I have counseled with thousands of people over the years, and I have noticed a common occurrence in their lives. (It's even true about my own life.) I've discovered that we all have little ships of sin, waiting in the harbors of our flesh, to carry us away from the will of God. I don't know what your "sin ships" are, but I know mine; and if we are going to really make history for the glory of God, then it's going to require this same kind of radical commitment, we see in Cortés. We need to burn the ships! We must burn the ships of lust, pride, procrastination, selfishness, and any other sinful ships harbored in our flesh that will cause us to turn-back from our allegiance to the Lord. Here's the good news, we *can* burn them! As believers in Jesus, we have the Holy Spirit in us, Who gives us power over our flesh. This is great news for us, because through His power, we can torch anything that waits to lure

us away from our new life in Christ.

Chapter Nineteen

Assurance

Our new life in-Christ brings with it some incredible benefits. One of them is unwrapped in the last part of this nugget we call Proverbs 3:6. Solomon said, "He shall direct your paths." What an amazing promise!

The power behind this whole promise begins with the word, "He." The significance is not that it's a third-person, singular, personal pronoun. That's true, but the essence of the word, "He," is what delivers the power for this promise. According to the syntax of this text, "He" is speaking about Jehovah, and it's crucial to remember that He is a faithful, covenant-keeping God. Solomon is saying that if we have done these three steps, then our actions evoke the activity of God in our lives in a powerful way. This means, if we attach ourselves to God, avoid our own logic, and acknowledge the Lord, then, we will have an assurance in our lives. This assurance is that He will direct our paths.

The promise is that He's going to do something. He is intervening on our behalves. He begins advancing supernatural abilities, to overcome our disabilities. When we adhere to the Lord, avoiding our own fleshly logic, acknowledging the Lord, He commences an intervention-plan in our lives. This news grabs my attention, as it should yours. Think about it. — The God, Who is holding the world, suspended in nothingness by the Word of His power, is saying that He is going to act on our behalves! Do you feel the optimism dripping like honey off of these words of hope?

Solomon clearly tells us how God is going to interpose His power over our problems: "He shall direct your paths." The word "direct" is a verb, and it means to make straight. The word "paths" simply refers to a road. There are metaphorical overtones in this phrase. Obviously, God is not saying that as you drive or walk down a literal, winding road, He will step-in, and with a miraculous act of engineering, your road will be straight as an arrow. That's not it, at all. Defined by theologians, this arrangement of words assures us that God will manage the affairs of our lives. For every issue we face, He stands ready to intervene in our problems, and He will do so in such a way, that those who are watching us will see the grand story of God unfolding before their eyes. He is carrying His precious loved-ones through the trials and tribulations of this sin-cursed world, safely over to the other side.

If you have read my book, Hurt Healer, then you know that I had a very sad relationship with my adopted father. In a lot of ways, he was a good man, but he had a violent side, that I saw more times, than I care to remember. He had great weaknesses in the areas of anger and verbal abuse. He often told me that he wished he would have never adopted me. Those words crushed me, and they damaged my heart on multiple levels. One adverse result was the way they perverted my perspective of God, as my Father. This warped thinking caused me to question everything I heard about God. When

I read this proverb, I thought, "Yeah, right." You see, I had a hard time trusting my earthly dad, and it jacked-up my trust in God, as my Heavenly Dad. I thought God couldn't be trusted. If you have been hurt by someone, then chances are, you will struggle with trust issues, as well. Satan would love to take that pain and use it to rob us of God's promises. I'm not going to let that happen to you.

One helpful exercise I did to overcome this issue, was to simply check-out God's track record. That's right, just go back over the Bible, find some individuals, who had to trust God; and I put them on the witness stand. That's what I did. Court was in order, and God's trustworthiness was on-trial.

The first witness I called to the stand was Moses. As I read through the pages of Exodus chapter fourteen, the answer began to come. On their journey out of slavery and into the Promise Land, the Hebrews found themselves faced with a ginormous problem. They were stuck—behind them lay a range of mountains and a vast, barren desert; before them, sprawled a massive sea, with no way to cross it; and Pharaoh's army was hotly advancing from behind, to take them back into slavery. The people began to complain to Moses about the situation, and Moses called out to God for help. God spoke and told him to lift up his rod and stretch out his hand over the sea.

Could you imagine being the leader, with the people asking, "Hey, did God give you a game plan?" Your reply, "Yes, He did." Big smiles spread across their faces. "Great! What is it?" they asked. Your brain is telling you not to share it, but you blurt out, "He told me to raise this stick up over the water." What kind of response do you think that would get? Probably something like, "Ask Him if He has a better plan!"

Moses, being a man of God, did not *lean unto his own understanding*; but instead, he *acknowledged God*, and God directed him and His people right through the Red Sea! I put him on the stand, and Moses' answer was clear: God can be trusted!

Even after that story, I found that I still needed more evidence, so I called Daniel to the stand. He was a Jew, taken captive by the Babylonians, in 606 BC. He was a devout man, full of faith in Jehovah-God. Later in his life, his commitment to God landed him in a perplexing situation. Because he prayed to Jehovah, and not to King Darius of the Persians, he was thrown into a den of lions, to be eaten alive. He prayed and found himself in a major, life-threatening problem, so he qualifies as a perfect guy to ask, if God can be trusted. The answer came in Daniel 6:22, "My God sent His angel and shut the lions' mouths, so that they have not hurt me." Can you imagine that? What was it like to hear their hungry growls, and to see their flesh-ripping fangs? How much tighter did he crouch in-prayer, when he felt the beasts' hot breath sweep across his neck? Could you imagine how joyful the moment was, when the lion, which he thought would eat him, instead playfully licked his face? What elation warmed his soul, as the monster-cats curled-up around him, creating the warmest, coziest bed he'd ever slept on? — He may have never gotten a better night's sleep in his life! Daniel's answer is clear: God can be trusted.

What about those, who went through problems, and it did *not* turn out so well? The Apostle Paul was beheaded, as was John the Baptist. Many of the other disciples were martyred. What about

God's faithfulness, when it comes to *their* lives? Can He be trusted? To answer that question, I invited Jesus Christ to the witness stand, Who also had a moment of tension with His Father.

Knowing the Cross was coming, Jesus was praying, and, in Matthew 26:39, He said, "O My Father, if it is possible, let this cup pass." There is no rebellion or push-back going on between Father and Son. Jesus was a human; He felt what was coming and was wrestling with what He had to face. Yet, He yielded His desire to be protected from suffering, and declared, "Nevertheless, not as I will, but as You will." Later that night and into the next day, He took our punishment for our sins and was butchered on a cross. As He hung there in excruciating pain, Mark 15:34 tells us that He cried out, "My God, My God, why have You forsaken Me?"

(There are thousands of smart theologians, who have weighed-in on what was happening in that moment. They know way more than I do, so I'll let them make all the heavy-definitive commentaries on those words. I just want us to think about the obvious.) It's totally clear that Jesus felt like He had been abandoned in His time of trouble, so He cried out! —Haven't we all?

What I love about this peek into Christ's humanity, is what we see happening, even for those who struggle. God showed Himself faithful. You may be thinking I have lost my mind here, because Jesus died a cruel death. Yes, He did, but what happened three days later? He arose! The resurrection of Jesus Christ is all the proof we need that God, the Covenant-Keeper, *can be trusted.* Yes, He may bring us through our troubles, like He did for Moses and Daniel; but it might just be that we suffer from the fall-out of a sin-cursed world so deeply, that it costs us our lives. What then? —We can look to Jesus, and let it fuel our faith. As 2 Corinthians 4:14 says, "Knowing that He, Who raised up the Lord Jesus will also raise us up with Jesus." It may not turn-out the way we planned it, or would like for it to go, but God can be trusted!

Chapter Twenty

Heaven

We started with a little time-machine trip, now let's end it with one. Hop-in with me, and I'll turn the space-travel knob forward. Let's take a leap into your future. How far into the future? I've set the time indicator to ten thousand years from now.

Knowing that God will raise us up one day, like He raised up Jesus, means that we will live forever with God in Heaven. Our journey through this book has led us to understand that those, who have a proper belief in Jesus, who have "gotten into the wheel-barrow," will be admitted into Heaven. This is great news! Let's go see just how marvelous it is.

We will die one day, but death is merely the transportation we use to get to Heaven. Although death is the end of life, as we know it on earth, it's the start of eternal life in Heaven. The Bible is clear about the fact that we will live forever. John 3:16 states it well; we won't perish, but we'll have everlasting life. Paul, in 1 Corinthians 15, gives us some great insight about our resurrection. He says, "We shall be changed. For this corruptible must put on incorruption, and this mortal must put on immortality. So, when this corruptible has put on incorruption, and this mortal has put on immortality, then shall be brought to pass the saying that is written: 'Death is swallowed up in victory.' 'O Death, where is your sting? O Hades, where is your victory?'"

Do you see it? Death is not the end for the believer; it's the dawning of a new life. II Corinthians 5:8 says, "We are confident, yes, well-pleased, rather, to be absent from the body and to be present with the Lord." One day, we will be with the Lord Jesus, but what will that look like? What will it be like? I don't have all the answers for that. There are some great minds that have written some awesome books about Heaven; but I do have one thing that I have learned about it, and it fires me up. Perhaps, it will do the same for you. Since we are in our time- machine, let's buckle-up, and let's warp-on-over to the other side.

Remember the story back in Luke 16, about the rich man and the beggar? When Jesus told that story it was much like the verses we have looked at in Matthew chapter seven. He is opening a portal that crosses us into a whole, different dimension of time and space. He takes us into eternity. We referenced these verses earlier and gave a lot of attention to the man, who went to Hell. Now we are going to look at the other man in this story, the beggar.

I want to make a note here about the story. Just like I think the Good Samaritan story and the events of Matthew 7:21-23 are actual events, I'm inclined to believe that the story of the rich man and the beggar was, too. The thing that tips me in this direction of thought, is the fact that Jesus calls a guy in the story by name. He says the man's name is Lazarus. It may not be that significant, but it doesn't happen in any of the other parables. I think this is an actual event that actually happened, to actual people. This is important, because if that's the case, then what happened to them, could actually happen to us. Let's check out what happened to the beggar.

One day, when the dogs came to lick the beggar's sores, they found his skin shockingly cold; He was dead. Jesus says that when the beggar died—and I love this—the angels came and carried him to Abraham's bosom. It's comforting to know that when we step out of this life, there are loving angels to meet us and to escort us into the after-life. Hebrews 1:14 tells us that angels are "spirits sent forth to minister for those who will inherit salvation." This proved to be true for the beggar, as they were there for him at his hour of passing, but where exactly did they take him?

Jesus said that they carried him to Abraham's bosom, but what is that all about? To understand the significance of this, you have to get into the head of the average Jewish person of Christ's day. They got the picture right off-the-bat, because Abraham's bosom was a Jewish figurative expression equivalent to Paradise. We have an account of Jesus using the term, "Paradise," while He was on the Cross. A thief was being executed next to Him and had placed his faith in Jesus. In Luke 23:43, we see Jesus looking at the thief and saying, "Today you will be with Me in Paradise." Christ was speaking about Heaven. This helps us to understand that the angels took the beggar to Heaven.

I should note here, that the man did not go to Heaven because he was a beggar; he went to Heaven because he was a believer. Only those, who authentically believe, get access into Heaven. That's where we find him, and I want you to notice something. This is the thing that thrills me about Heaven. Take a look at the story, yourself. After you have read it, do a little rewinding. Do you recall what the rich man was begging for in Hell? That's correct, he was begging for water. He was also begging that his loved ones would be warned about Hell's reality. Before he died, he never had to ask for water; his servants were waiting on him, hand and foot. If he needed to get news to someone, he could hire the best, securest courier on the planet. Now, in Hell, he is reduced to being a beggar. So tragic!

Now, take a look at the beggar, who is in Heaven. What kind of requests do we see him making? What's that? Could you say that a little louder? I'm sorry, I could not hear you. Yes, that's correct, he is asking for *nothing*. I find this absolutely marvelous! On earth, he was fighting for his life, kicking the dogs back from eating away at his sores, as his stomach growled for just a small bit of crumbs from the rich man's table. Now, in Heaven, he has no wants and is satisfied completely. What a glorious picture of the future that awaits all of us, who have placed our faith in Jesus!

Our time-machine has stopped! We are now in Heaven. Remember, we took this trip to see what your life is going to look like in the future. You have been here for ten thousand years, and for the infinite thousands of years to come, like the beggar, you will always be without want. Imagine that! It's just as Revelation said it would be in chapter twenty-one and verse four, "And God will wipe away every tear from their eyes; there shall be no more death, nor sorrow, nor crying. There shall be no more pain, for the former things have passed away." You haven't had anything to cry about for ten thousand years. You haven't experienced one tiny moment of sorrow; there hasn't been a funeral or a sickness. You haven't had one single morning, when you had to get up and go to work, and there aren't bills piling-up in your mailbox.

All the people you live around, and those you hang-out with, love each other unconditionally; there are no grudges, insults, or conflicts. There are no wars, no earthquakes, no tornados, and no terrorism! You are in Heaven, basking in the glory of God and enjoying the blessings He has prepared for you that nothing can ever corrupt, take away, or destroy. This has all been made possible only through the salvation that God offered you. It's His gift to you! The anthem of the saints, sung on Sundays in churches throughout the world, could never do it justice; yet, now, you know of its truth, as proclaimed in John Newton's "Amazing Grace"—

"Yea, when this flesh and heart shall fail,

And mortal life shall cease,

I shall possess within the veil,

A life of joy and peace.

When we've been here ten thousand years

Bright shining as the sun,

We've no less days to sing God's praise

Than when we've first begun."

Closing Thought

A young lady walked into a small convenient store and thought she would try her luck at one of the scratch-off lottery card games. She bought a card that had six boxes on it. To play, you simply scratch-off three boxes. To win, you must have matching numbers in all three boxes. Using her fingernail, she scratched-off the first box, and it read, "25k." Not hopeful at all, she rubbed-off the thin layer of silver paint from the second box, which also revealed, "25k." With her heart pounding, she randomly scratched another tiny square. To her amazement, it was another "25k!" She was a WINNER! You can imagine how excited she was. Thrilled to have finally won, she went to the official lottery headquarters to cash-in on her winnings.

She waited in a small line, and once it was her turn, she handed the card to the clerk behind the counter. "I'm a winner!" she exclaimed. The attendant smiled, looked at the card, and asked her to wait, while he went to secure her winnings. Several minutes went by, and he returned. She stuck-out her hand to receive the money, and he placed her ticket in her palm. "What's up with that? Where's my money?" she blurted. The clerk frowned and replied, "Ma'am, I am so sorry, but I can't give you the money. The card is a misprint." How depressing! One second she's queen-bank, and the next, she's back to dog-broke. That would be a very disheartening moment.

I want you to read the following lines very carefully, and then pay close attention to what I say afterward.

'Trust in the Lord with all of your heart,

And lean not unto your own understanding;

In all your ways acknowledge Him,

And He shall direct your paths."

Hold-on to your coffee, I've got some great news for you. Those twenty-eight words are not a misprint! God placed every one of them in the Bible, and it would be foolish for you not to cash-in on them! God stands ready to deliver on His promise, so go for it! You're "in the wheelbarrow," and the capable hands of God will carry you through this life. Get ready to scoot-over, because you're going to tell this story so well, that your family, friends, neighbors, and co-workers are going to want to get in the wheelbarrow with you. I am among the throngs of other believers cheering you on!